W9-ATN-015

PhilanthropyRoundtable

Learning to Be Useful

A Wise Giver's Guide to Supporting Career and Technical Education

By David Bass

Copyright © 2016, The Philanthropy Roundtable. All rights reserved.

Published by The Philanthropy Roundtable, 1120 20th Street NW, Suite 550 South, Washington, D.C. 20036

Free copies of this book are available to qualified donors. To learn more, or to order more copies, call (202) 822-8333, e-mail main@PhilanthropyRoundtable.org, or visit PhilanthropyRoundtable.org. Printed and e-book versions are available from major online booksellers. A PDF may be downloaded at no charge at PhilanthropyRoundtable.org.

No part of this publication may be reproduced, stored in a retrieval system, or transmitted in any form or by any means, electronic, mechanical, photocopying, recording, scanning, or otherwise, except as permitted under Section 107 or 108 of the 1976 U.S. Copyright Act, without the written permission of The Philanthropy Roundtable. Requests for permission to reprint or otherwise duplicate should be sent to main@PhilanthropyRoundtable.org.

Cover: © Krystian Nawrocki/istockphoto.com

ISBN 978-0-9861474-6-3
LCCN 2016949479

First printing, September 2016

Current Wise Giver's Guides from The Philanthropy Roundtable

Karl Zinsmeister, *series editor*
For all current and future titles, visit PhilanthropyRoundtable.org/guidebook

TABLE OF CONTENTS

PREFACE

The Double Payoff from Enhanced Career and Technical Education

Last year, The Philanthropy Roundtable published a guidebook that identifies powerful strategies and top organizations that donors can use to help economic strugglers finally get a solid footing in the job market. After explaining how important work is to self-image and social life as well as economic success, that book provides rich practical information about how marginal populations like the homeless, single mothers on welfare, former addicts, former prisoners, the disabled, and high-school dropouts can be drawn into solid entry-level jobs where they can succeed and establish stable lives. Entitled *Clearing Obstacles to Work: A Wise Giver's Guide to Fostering Self-Reliance*, the book is available on Amazon or in bulk from the Roundtable offices.

The volume you are about to read is a natural follow-on to that predecessor. This guide will help philanthropists make public contributions toward one of today's most hotly debated issues—improving the upward mobility of low-income workers. The key to helping entry-level employees gain more responsibility and enough income to support a family is to raise their skill level. The biggest opportunity is in so-called "middle-skill" jobs that don't require a college education but do require some formal postsecondary training. This training is often capped by a competency test of some sort that makes sure you really do know how to run a computer-controlled lathe, or field customer service phone calls, or weld underwater, or hook up a computer network.

The thrill of using career and technical education to prepare new cohorts of Americans for middle-skill responsibilities is that you can be part of a double payoff. You'll help unleash economic mobility for marginalized populations. And at the same time you'll stoke our national economic engine. The quiet secret of industrial America is that many businesses and industries now face crippling shortages of technical workers. Philanthropic alliances with businesses and educators to create new training pathways are one of today's most promising ways of helping our nation and its people.

We thank the Lenfest, Achelis, and Dr. Phillips foundations for generous funding that made this book possible.

The Philanthropy Roundtable exists to help donors succeed in strengthening our nation in the ways they deem most useful and important. If we can help your charitable efforts to expand economic opportunity and deepen U.S. prosperity, please let us know.

Jo Kwong
Director of Economic Opportunity Programs

Adam Meyerson
President
The Philanthropy Roundtable

INTRODUCTION

Donors Can Open Pathways to Prosperity

What kind of education does it take to obtain a middle-class wage in America today? The answer might surprise you.

On the one hand, the days of earning a living with only a high-school diploma are waning. Young adults with just a high-school diploma have a poverty rate of 22 percent today. That compares to 7 percent in 1979.

While offshoring and trade are often blamed for the decline of working-class opportunities, the fact is that U.S. manufacturing is actually *increasing* its output. Technological advancements, however, are enabling machines to replace low-skilled jobs. This means that working-class life can no longer be solidly built on toil alone—skills are required. A 2012 report by Georgetown University's Public Policy Institute summarizes: "In the postindustrial economy, the notion of a muscular working class has gone the way of U.S. Steel, displaced by a new class of working families in postindustrial jobs that require at least some college."

The conventional response to this trend is to push a four-year bachelor's degree for everyone, more or less assuming job prospects on the other side will take care of themselves. And today's college infrastructure is largely built to push young people toward a bachelor's over any other credential.

The unfortunate result is that many youths are prodded onto a traditional college path they are unprepared and unsuited for, leading to high dropout rates and a growing number of Americans with some college experience—and debt—but no completed degree. This approach has also failed adults in low-wage jobs who want to boost their economic prospects but can't realistically devote four to six years to earning a degree that might or might not improve their earning potential. The result is that for many working adults, college is a failed and financially costly experience that doesn't lead to useful credentials or improved life outcomes. Even some of those who persist all the way to a bachelor's degree discover it isn't a guaranteed path to economic prosperity. And employers find that in an era where four-year college degrees are diluted and pushed on everyone, this traditional proxy for skills and knowledge isn't as valuable as it once was.

Yet, strikingly, there is a growing pool of jobs today—to the tune of 29 million—that require what academics call "middle skills." These skills are generally conferred by apprenticeships or organized postsecondary education other than a bachelor's degree. Persons capable of doing these jobs are in many places sought hungrily by employers, and the positions pay enough to launch any steadily working family head into the middle class.

Despite attractive salaries and benefits, employers in many places are experiencing shortages of workers qualified for middle-skill jobs—particularly in fields like health care, advanced manufacturing, and energy. To keep their labor pipelines filled, employers such as Toyota and ExxonMobil have created their own training and credentialing programs, or have partnered with local community colleges and nonprofits for this purpose. Other smaller businesses have created apprenticeships or worked with nonprofits to pull high-school graduates into programs that will leave them qualified for positions like electrician or stonemason. General appreciation of the breadth of middle-skill opportunities, however, remains low. Businesses and low-skill workers alike need help erecting programs that can bridge this economic gap.

Unfortunately, career and technical education has an image problem. In some circles technical education is associated with blue-collar jobs without much upside, reflecting the old-style vocational education that often relegated "non-college-ready" students to dead-end, low paying jobs. With many K-12 schools defining success simply by the number of students they send to four-year colleges, the bias against career education can be pronounced.

"If all we do is send the message that it's college or bust, we're not really giving the right kind of opportunities to everybody," says Chauncy Lennon, who leads JPMorgan Chase's philanthropic workforce development initiatives. Nicholas Wyman of the Institute for Workplace Skills and Innovation confirms that even though programs now exist that give students stellar credentials and career prospects, technical training remains anathema to some. "Today, high-schoolers hear barely a whisper about the many doors that the vocational education path can open."

Enter private philanthropy. For the past year I've been researching the best donor-funded efforts throughout the nation focused on connecting workers with opportunities to enter the middle class. These programs make sure workers are job-ready in a basic sense, confirming they have the entry-level skills that were the focus of our previous guidebook *Clearing Obstacles to Work: A Wise Giver's Guide to Fostering Self-Reliance*. But the programs included in this book then offer something more: detailed, sometimes complex, technical education that equips workers for a rewarding career and greater upward mobility.

Some of the existing efforts are broad and national. For example, JPMorgan Chase has committed $250 million over five years to further define and disseminate middle-skill career pathways. The Lumina Foundation is using an endowment of over $1 billion to help raise to 60 percent by 2025 the percentage of Americans with a high-quality postsecondary degree. These larger initiatives employ a variety of means—national gatherings where standards are set and needs are identified, collaborations between companies and educators, public campaigns and advocacy—to advance their missions.

The Bill & Melinda Gates Foundation has become involved in ways ranging from providing financial aid to collecting important data. Gates is also trying to strengthen the public image of alternative career pathways by funding research incubators like Jobs for the Future and the ACT Foundation.

> Today, young adults with only a high-school diploma have a poverty rate of 22 percent. That compares to 7 percent in 1979.

But movement-building is just one way for donors to get involved. Philanthropists are also working hard to raise STEM job awareness in high school, arrange internships with area employers, and pay for the research to understand current job opportunities and the corresponding skills necessary, among many other interventions and incremental improvements.

An example at the local level is the Pinkerton Foundation, which directs $14 million in annual giving to support career-internship opportunities, industry-specific certifications, and rigorous job-training programs that teach both the hard and soft skills needed to advance in the workplace. Focusing on at-risk youth in the New York City region, Pinkerton encourages trainers to work closely with local employers so the skill sets developed are in line with available local jobs.

Many other foundations are making similar investments in young people. The Benedum Foundation is focusing on blue-collar workers in West Virginia and southwestern Pennsylvania, even embedding career academies into high schools. In the City of Brotherly Love, the Lenfest Foundation supports Penn Medicine's volunteer programs for adults, college students, and teens. Students as young as 14 can volunteer over the summer at the university's hospital, gaining exposure to well-paid careers in medicine that are currently short of qualified applicants.

Business leaders are also getting involved. In Houston, local businessman Beau Pollock needed more electricians for his enterprise and started a direct relationship with YES Prep and his local KIPP charter schools. Now students showing interest in the electric profession can work directly with his company out of high school. Robert Luddy—a donor, entrepreneur, and founder of CaptiveAire Systems (America's leading supplier of kitchen ventilation systems)—has woven apprenticeships both into his business and into his network of private schools in North Carolina. "Apprenticeship is the best of all worlds," says Luddy, stressing the importance of on-the-job experience. As sophomores, students in Luddy's Thales Academy can obtain a certificate in SolidWorks, which alone would enable them to make between $40,000 and $60,000 in the marketplace.

Recently deceased donor and Intel co-founder Andrew Grove carved his niche in career and technical education by offering scholarships. He typically gave out 100 stipends per year to students in community college who were transitioning directly to the workforce rather than a four-year school. Grove found that improvements in community college curricula and delivery are an excellent mechanism for training the next generation of middle-skill workers.

For example, take Rio Salado College in Tempe, Arizona. Rio Salado educates more than 57,000 students at any given time—30,000 of whom are accessing all of their instruction online. It's the largest online community college in the U.S., and has classes that start on 48 dates all throughout the year—an especially attractive feature for adult learners. The college offers a vast variety of programs—mobile apps programming, infant and toddler development, dental assisting, quality customer service, small business startup, and paralegal. With the help of the Gates Foundation and other donors, Rio Salado has peer donors, career coaches, and other support for learners to make sure that its programming matches available well-paying jobs needed in the community.

Another promising example with a slightly different twist is Valencia College in Orlando, Florida. Leaders at the college have found that a traditional academic model—here's a list of classes, take a few over two or so years—isn't working well for career advancement. So instead, Valencia is doubling down and accelerating many of its programs to take around five weeks. These short bursts of training are ideal for adults who are already working. "If we take them through a series of very short tunnels, where the opportunity cost of lost wages while they're in school is small, they're perfectly willing to enroll," says Valencia president Sandy Shugart. Accelerated tracks are focused on obtaining a "stackable" credential that, in various combinations, leads to progressively higher paying jobs. Valencia's most popular tracks are in nursing, cardiovascular technology, engineering technologies, entertainment-related technologies, criminal justice, and paralegal work.

In addition to accelerated options, Valencia works with its local Goodwill branches to provide services like child care and transportation for students who need them—eliminating common obstacles that prevent students from persisting all the way to a useful credential. Funding partner organizations that offer these supports and keep students on track, says Shugart, is one of the most valuable roles philanthropy can play. But he stresses that the best way to mitigate some of these barriers is to keep the program short—the longer the program, the more likely that something will come up.

Shugart describes Orlando as a juxtaposition between two economies—high-tech prosperous jobs and low-skilled, low paying ones. "We have the most powerful economy in the world for putting unskilled people into low-paying jobs," he says. "The problem is that these jobs are hard to move up from. It takes two body lengths to reach the next rung on the ladder. So our strategy has been to add more rungs to the ladder. We have lots of people in our community who need a very short burst of training that will move their value to an employer by $2 an hour or more."

This concept of putting more rungs on the ladder, or "upskilling," is gaining traction among workforce nonprofits, community colleges, and employers. The dozens of donors, experts, and nonprofit practitioners I interviewed on this subject coalesced around a number of common practices where philanthropists can clearly help. These will be explored in more detail in Chapter 8, but here are a few broad areas for you to be thinking about as you read the following pages and try to envision where your organization can be most helpful:

1. Create clear pathways. Career mapping is essential, because adult workers need a discernible return on investment before they are willing to enroll in a program. Successful programs demonstrate

each step a student needs to take to complete the program for a credential and embark on an upward career path.

2. Condense timeframes and increase schedule flexibility. Many candidates for "middle-skill" training are already in an entry-level job and helping support a household, so long periods out of the workforce are not practical. Accelerated programs are thus very useful and attractive. In some cases, nine-month classes are being compressed into 16-week bursts. Low-income workers who can't afford to take a year off for education might be able to swing intensive evening classes for four months.

3. Overcome negative perceptions about higher education. Low-income workers might not view themselves as able to successfully swim in the waters of postsecondary education. Effective programs inspire their students and affirm that completing the credential is possible and expected.

4. Acknowledge and account for remedial learners. Some adult learners face the basic roadblock of lacking skills in the basics of reading, writing, and arithmetic. Accelerated programs to bring them up to speed are essential to completing higher credentials.

5. Offer student services that make class attendance easier. The McKinsey Social Initiative has found that distance to class is the top indicator of whether a new arrival in a training class will persist. Transportation obstacles are serious. Addressing practical hurdles like these can often make or break an adult learner's success.

Partly thanks to creative help from donors, the field of career and technical education is ready for a renaissance. Students, communities, and philanthropists willing to invest in career and technical education may be pleasantly surprised at how much difference they can make. "This isn't your grandfather's vocational education," says Lucretia Murphy of Jobs for the Future, a national nonprofit expanding workforce opportunities. "These are good jobs. These are well-paying jobs. These are jobs that put people in line for promotions. These are jobs that are fulfilling."

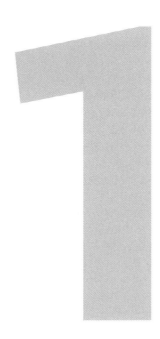

Why Technical Training Will Boost Upward Mobility

Stagnating wages. Gaps between rich and poor. Anemic labor-force participation. Stalled economic mobility. These are hot buttons in America today. The Pew Research Center recently startled many observers with a report that the combination of low-income households plus high-income households now outnumbers our middle class, the vaunted backbone of the United States.

Philanthropists know that our nation's economy can do better. How can they help?

First they have to understand today's issues accurately. One of the most mourned developments of the modern era is the stranding of millions of blue-collar workers on the economic margins. Unskilled or low-skilled men have seen their real wages decline 28 percent since 1980. Significant numbers of workers who once were proudly independent are now living on disability payments, food stamps, Medicaid, and other welfare benefits. Young people without skills see few routes to a career that can raise a family.

International competition and new technology mean that labor once done by human brawn is now assigned to machines. Contrary to some perceptions, America's manufacturing economy has grown strongly. While our manufacturers have shed 7 million jobs since the 1970s, their output has climbed to over $2 trillion of products annually. The U.S. economic engine churns out more things and more value than ever before. But the employees it needs now are ones with specialized skills, or the ability to adapt and learn new tasks as work mutates.

Seven out of ten jobs today require at least some kind of training beyond high-school—a certificate, occupational credential, or degree. Due to a combination of new positions and openings due to retirement, millions of work slots open up every year now. Most of the positions that provide a middle-class wage, however, require some kind of specialized knowledge.

Government responses to today's struggles among the working class have mostly been to funnel more money into unemployment compensation, welfare programs, social services, and disability compensation. While providing short-term salve to the wounded, these responses actually perpetuate economic malaise in the long run. The longer someone stays out of the workforce on long-term unemployment or disability, the less likely they are to ever land a good job again.

Meanwhile, some well-intentioned philanthropists, educators, and reformers have insisted that today's need for specialized skills means everyone must go to college for four years. Americans who could thrive with the right dose of career and technical education are instead pigeonholed into booklearning and a multiyear college experience they cannot afford, do not need, and often will not complete.

A bias for the bachelor's degree

Just from 2000 to 2010, enrollment at public four-year colleges increased by 34 percent. Many of those enrollees made good use of their college experience. Many floundered.

In many ways, today's educational infrastructure is built to push young people into four-year bachelor's degrees. In the 2013-2014 school year, 74 percent of federal Pell grants went to students aiming for at least a bachelor's degree. Only 22 percent went to students planning on an associate degree, and just 4 percent went to students pursuing an occupational certificate.

The U.S. bias for bachelor's degrees is very different from the pattern in may other advanced nations. OECD data show that the U.S. ranks second in baccalaureate attainment, but only 16th in postsecondary attainment below a bachelor's degree. This preference is influencing U.S. competitiveness. The U.S. "is an outlier in focusing on postsecondary completion rather than on education having as its primary purpose to help young people find a calling or vocation," writes workforce expert Nancy Hoffman in *Schooling in the Workplace*.

Seven out of ten jobs today require some kind of training beyond high school—a certificate, occupational credential, or degree.

Many young Americans are being prodded into traditional college courses they are unprepared and unsuited for. This leads to high dropout rates and a growing number of young people with some college experience but no completed degree. And it leaves in the cold many older adults who hold low-wage jobs and hunger for more responsibility and pay, but cannot take a multiyear detour from household responsibilities to go to university. "We need to move away from this one-trick-pony model of a four-year degree for all," says Drexel University labor economist Paul Harrington.

"A four-year school," agrees Dennis Dio Parker, is "not the only pathway." That, he says, is just "a middle-class myth." Parker is head of Toyota's Advanced Manufacturing Program, an initiative profiled later in this guidebook which creates employment opportunities for young people interested in skilled technical trades. It offers three interlinked job courses. Enrollees can be schooled as a skilled technician or in engineering, or given business training. This effort has helped ensure that Toyota has a strong human-talent stream for its factories. And it has qualified thousands of participants for high-wage employment.

"We're pushing all these kids into four-year liberal arts. They have all this debt. They don't have the aptitude for it. So they end up driving cabs...or tending bar, or unemployed and living with their parents.... Whereas they may have great aptitudes as an electrician or mechanic, making $100,000 a year." So says Charles Koch, in describing a new top priority of his foundation. "Some of them with that aptitude start their own businesses. They become wealthy because they are satisfying a real need, not because somebody subsidized them and pushed them into things they can't really make a contribution in."

Not just young people from lower-income families but also many from solidly middle-class backgrounds are struggling under today's exaggerated focus on a four-year degree as the educational gold standard. Ask the counterperson at your local coffee house about his or her economic background and you are likely to get a very personal glimpse of this dynamic. Learning that a bachelor's degree is no guarantee of economic success can be painful for unsuspecting college graduates. Unless more forms of postsecondary education with clear pathways into careers are established and widely advertised, growing numbers of young people will be burned by this discovery in the future.

Even if it doesn't result in out-and-out unemployment, many college-trained youth now experience a disconnect between their choice of major and employer demands in the workforce. Of the five most popular fields of college study today, only one (health professions and related programs) falls within the category where employers say they are most frantically undersupplied with adequate workers—so-called STEM jobs (science, technology, engineering, and math). Between 2010 and 2020, the U.S. "will produce twice as many graduates in social sciences and business as in science, technology, engineering, and mathematics," reports the McKinsey Global Initiative, "exacerbating the shortage of qualified candidates for technical jobs."

Employers flooded with applicants bearing fuzzy and often very soft bachelor's degrees are finding they need to focus on past work experience and demonstrated competencies, as proxies for skills and knowledge, more than on educational degrees. This is not a matter of employers being overly picky, says Andy Van Kleunen of the National Skills Coalition, but rather of workers lacking basic skills necessary for the real jobs that companies now need to fill. A four-year college degree doesn't translate the way it once did.

In his 2013 book *College (Un)bound*, higher-ed expert Jeffrey Selingo summarizes trends this way:

> Over the last 30 years—and particularly in the first decade of the new millennium—American higher education has lost its way. At the very top, the most elite and prestigious institutions remain the best—the world still clamors to get into Harvard, Princeton, Yale, Berkeley, Stanford, Amherst, Williams, and a few dozen other household brands. But at the colleges and universities attended by most American students, costs are spiraling out of control and quality is declining just as increasing international competition demands that higher education be more productive and less expensive. Only slightly more than 50 percent of American students who enter college leave with a bachelor's degree. Among wealthy countries, only Italy ranks lower. As a result, the United States is now ranked number twelve among developed nations in higher-education attainment by its young people. As the baby boomer generation leaves the workforce, the country risks having successive generations less educated than the ones that preceded them for the first time.

For a sizable portion of the American population, pursuing a bachelor's degree now leads to poor outcomes. The college-for-all slogan has produced a triple punch of high student-loan debt obligations, high incomplete-degree rates, and weak career prospects. At the same time, a high-school diploma alone is now inadequate to assure a middle-class standard of living.

Do alternatives exist? Savvy philanthropists, business owners, educators, and workforce reformers know the answer: Yes.

Career and technical education—a yawning opportunity

Lost amid the mania that would push every American toward a bachelor's degree is an essential middle ground: a credential that is more than a high-school diploma, but less than a four-year degree, and that focuses tightly on technical skills in immediate demand in the marketplace. The currently favored lingo for such training is career and technical education (CTE). CTE integrates education with workforce development and leaves graduates capable of filling the "middle-skill" jobs that are in high demand in our new economy, and that pay family-sustaining wages. It's an arena that experts agree holds exceptional promise both for reviving America's working class, and for kickstarting our national economic engine. And donors have wide opportunities to be productive here.

A generation ago, "vocational education" was the term of art. We will use that shorthand occasionally in this book. But the low quality of some previous vocational education has given that term a negative connotation for some educators. Vocational ed was sometimes simply what was offered to weak students, after crude assessment by aptitude test (or, worse, by race). High scorers would be tracked to college prep classes. Low scorers would be dumped into work-training programs that often were not very ambitious or particularly well taught. This is one source of today's unwise insistence in places on "college or bust."

This crude history eventually led to dried-up funding for vocational education. Since 2000 alone, funding for high-school vocational ed programs has declined by 15 to 20 percent. Career-focused education remains anathema to some educators, notes Nicholas Wyman of the Institute for Workplace Skills and Innovation. "The 'college-for-everyone' mentality has pushed awareness of other possible career paths to the margins," he recently wrote in *Forbes*. "The cost to the individuals and the economy as a whole is high."

Behind the scenes, however, private-sector donors and businesses have been quietly working, and making alliances together, to produce successful models of career-oriented education. Philanthropists have discovered, in CTE, a way to help individuals who otherwise would be stuck in an economic rut to achieve stable, middle-class lives. Employers and new job creators have found talented workers that they desperately need. And this alliance has unfolded in a low-cost, efficient manner, opening on-ramps to jobs for graduates relatively quickly and without painful political debates or social dislocations.

Blouke Carus—chairman emeritus of the Carus Corporation, a high-tech manufacturer in Illinois—argues that all U.S. youth should experience work-based learning, not just those in technical fields. In his decades as a donor and businessman, Carus has investigated European models of apprenticeship, engineering, and education reform, and worked to bring their lessons to American education. Among other advantages, "work-based learning motivates kids beyond belief," says Carus. "They see a future for their studying. They realize they if they read and write and figure and learn the sciences, a good life can unfold for them."

Carus has lots of company in drawing inspiration from successful European models of apprenticeships. Countries like Switzerland, Germany, and Austria have linked education and work in many ways, seamlessly integrating academics and vocation. Fully 70 percent of young people in Switzerland, 65 percent in Germany, and 55 percent in Austria are enrolled in apprenticeships. And all three countries have youth unemployment rates around half the U.S. level.

Robert Luddy—a donor, entrepreneur, and founder of CaptiveAire Systems, America's leading supplier of kitchen ventilation systems—has tightly woven apprenticeships into both his business and the network private schools he has created through his philanthropy in Wake County, North Carolina. As profiled later in this guidebook, Thales Academy operates a technology-intensive track for high-school students that has, as a focal point, a rigorous internship and apprenticing program.

Luddy is quick to answer when asked why apprenticeships are useful in a modern age:

> To form and develop individuals, you need mentors who can provide structured guidance. Some disciplines require traditional academic instruction for mastery. In other fields you have to learn directly under the supervision of vocational masters, because the task is nuanced, complicated, requires a specialized facility, or takes a long time to absorb. Whether you're learning to play the piano, or operate a business, or lay bricks, you really can't master it in a classroom. Mentors and various work experiences were foundational for me and helped me to grasp crucial concepts that weren't taught in school.

While acknowledging economic and cultural differences between the U.S. and European counterparts, advocates of apprenticeship like Luddy believe it is one of the easiest and surest ways we could improve the quality of our career education—and that it is a model where philanthropists working on a small scale can be especially helpful.

Thanks to active leadership from donors, old negative perceptions of career-oriented education are quickly being scrubbed away. "Manufacturing now involves higher pay and needs workers with higher skills," states Andi Korte, vice president of continuing education and workforce development at North Carolina's Sandhills Community College. "These are high-tech jobs. They earn respectable incomes doing important work."

Indeed, one of the philanthropic goals pursued by Karen Buchwald Wright, president and CEO of the Ohio-based Ariel Corporation, is to change the public perception of manufacturing. "Today's manufacturing is high-tech, high-skilled, and pays very well," she says. "It's a career path that can easily lead to management, if the person has the right attitude and aptitude."

Perhaps best of all, middle-skill jobs are plentiful in the American economy. Data compiled by the National Skills Coalition show that 54 percent of U.S. jobs fall into the middle-skill category. Low-skill jobs are now just 15 percent of our total. And 31 percent of U.S. jobs are high-skill.

Yet too few young people pursue middle-skill jobs, because they don't understand the opportunities they offer, or because they've bought into the four-year-degree-for-all mentality. And too few of the blue-collar adults who are struggling in today's job market are figuring out how to raise their skills to the middle level, in prompt and cost-effective ways. There is a big upside, with many beneficiaries, as this mismatch can be solved.

Many young Americans are being prodded into traditional college courses they are unprepared and unsuited for.

And there is reason to believe that more and better technical education could particularly revolutionize the educational experience of young men in America. Since the 1960s, educational trends have been zipping upward for females—who now significantly outnumber men on college campuses. But males have been suffering and declining on any number of educational measures. Equally, adult men have been getting battered in the labor force, with both rates of employment and levels of pay tumbling for many males.

Expanded tech-oriented training could help boys and men become more successful in K-12 education, in college, in job-winning, and in earnings trajectories—all the areas where males, especially blue-collar males, have been in eclipse. As the *Atlantic* pointed out in a 2013 article, "Young men may be a vanishing breed on the college campus, but there are some colleges that have no trouble attracting them—schools whose names include the letters T-E-C-H. Georgia Tech is 68 percent male;

Rochester Institute of Technology, 68 percent; South Dakota School of Mines and Technology, 74 percent. This affinity pattern points to one highly promising strategy for reconnecting boys with school...career and technical education."

First work, then prosperity

A previous guidebook in this series by The Philanthropy Roundtable was all about how donors can help disadvantaged Americans step onto the first rung of the economic ladder. *Clearing Obstacles to Work: A Wise Giver's Guide to Fostering Self-Reliance* explored hundreds of strategies for getting troubled youths, the homeless, former prisoners, disabled veterans, addicts, welfare-dependent single moms, and others into entry-level jobs. This 2015 guide showed that paid work—even of the simplest type—provides structure, stability, dignity, social interaction, and meaning, which is why heaps of evidence show that a job is a surer route out of poverty and unhappiness than any combination of social services. Philanthropic funders have become quite skilled in recent decades at introducing struggling populations to productive work, and helping them learn the basic skills needed to hold a job over the long haul.

For those coming out of poverty, incarceration, addiction, or dependence, a regular workplace and steady paycheck of any size will often be life-changing. But after an individual has reached that milestone, and proven he or she has mastered the disciplines and soft skills of being a useful worker, what's the next step? Staying for a long time in an entry-level job paying $8 to $10 per hour can make it hard to raise a family or achieve the security of a middle-class existence. The natural next step is to increase one's technical skills. Only with greater knowledge and abilities and technique can one command higher wages and a path upward.

If you're a donor already involved in opening doors to entry-level work, investing in career and technical education is a natural extension of your help. Excellent vocational education is needed to keep disadvantaged populations moving forward and upward. And it has the added benefit of helping businesses and local communities become more functional and successful. Technical education may be today's best tool for expanding America's vital middle class and boosting America's competitiveness.

Indeed, the authors of the Harvard Business School report *Bridge the Gap* call middle-skill jobs today's main "springboard" into middle-American prosperity. Individual donors, private foundations, and corporations are beginning to shift resources with this in mind.

Bret Halverson, an expert consultant on this topic, finds evidence that philanthropies and for-profit institutions are shifting some resources away from traditional education investments specifically so they can fatten their spending on CTE and workforce training.

Stagnating wages are a very appropriate concern for charitable action. Shortages of workers needed to keep American business strong are another very legitimate concern for public-spirited donors. Career education combats both negatives. Indeed, helping Americans become as productive as possible is a concern that goes back very far and very deep in the American experience. Benjamin Franklin, Peter Cooper, Julius Rosenwald, and many more of our greatest philanthropists placed this issue at the very center of their charitable concerns.

With the rise of high-quality career and technical education as a replacement for the mediocre vocational education of recent decades, many donors are showing signs of willingness to get back into this historic pursuit. Wise givers will of course want to see evidence of good results. A recent study from the Thomas B. Fordham Institute sheds some light on how positive the results in this area could be for learners. Using rich data from the Arkansas Research Center, this analysis followed more than 100,000 students from eighth grade through high school and into postsecondary education. It tracked which students took CTE courses and which didn't, then measured whether exposure to career and technical training brought tangible employment prospects to students. The results are heartening:

> In general, taking just one additional CTE course above the average increases a student's probability of graduating from high school by 3.2 percentage points, and of enrolling in a two-year college the following year by 0.6 percentage points. It also increases a student's probability of being employed the year after graduation by 1.5 percentage points, and boosts his or her expected quarterly wage that year by $28 (roughly 3 percent). Dual enrollment—earning college credit while still in high school—magnifies the impact of an additional CTE course by doubling the probability that a student will enroll in a two-year college the year after graduation. All of these differences are statistically significant.

This study found that low-income students were particularly likely to enjoy sturdy gains from exposure to career and technical education. Among lower-income students, for example, taking CTE classes made it 25 percent likelier the student would graduate from high school.

Simply put, giving to CTE programs is good philanthropy, because it's good for people. Here are seven specific ways that training Americans for middle-skill jobs benefits them:

Higher pay

Earning an associate degree will take a worker's earnings, on average, from $35,380 to $44,140 per year (in 2012 dollars), a nearly 25 percent increase. Other research shows that Americans with some college but no degree (some of whom might have an industry-recognized certificate) earn around $250,000 more over their lifetimes than those with a high-school diploma only. One analysis from California showed that CTE associate degrees produced a 25 percent bump in pay, and certificates led to a 10 percent jump.

> One analysis showed that associate degrees in career and technical fields produced a 25 percent bump in pay, and certificates a 10 percent bump.

Access to benefits

Middle-skill jobs are much more likely to be linked to health care and retirement savings vehicles.

Social mobility

Career and technical training provides qualifications that stack on top of previous competencies, gradually increasing earnings and building the market power of a worker. "Anybody can use stackable credentials to advance in a profession," notes Blouke Carus. "If an auto mechanic wants to go the next step and become a mechanical engineer or a process oper-ator or a chemical analyst, that's entirely possible."

Aligning schooling more appropriately with work

Many young people spend years in higher education that ultimately have little or no influence on their life in the workforce. This is wasteful and hurts both students and employers. The best CTE programs make sure that the dollars and hours students put into their schooling will bear fruit in their life that follows. "The world is not saying, 'Oh, you have a piece of paper? Sure, we'll hire you.' Specific skills and competencies are needed," summarizes Tom Riley of the Pennsylvania-based Connelly Foundation.

Making it easier to meld work and learning
CTE certificates, degrees, and certifications are often set up to be accessible to people who are actively working and supporting dependents. "We have lots of people in our community who need a very short burst of training to improve their value to employers—training that sometimes requires as little as three weeks, sometimes as much as 14 weeks, but rarely more than that," says Sandy Shugart, president of Valencia College in Orlando, a CTE-rich school profiled later in this guidebook.

The fact that apprenticeships, on-the-job-training, internships, and mentoring are so often part of CTE training is also very helpful to people already in the workforce. "Because CTE is career-focused, it has a unique advantage for working learners," write the authors of Georgetown University's 2012 report *Five Ways That Pay Along the Way to the B.A.* "In the short run, students with relevant knowledge and skills can secure positions that pay.... In the long run, students will have developed career-relevant skills and gained work experience that bring dividends as they advance their careers."

Lifelong learning
With a rapidly changing economy, career education is not something to be done for a few years then left behind. The most successful workers will keep learning and evolving in their skills to remain competitive. Nimbleness, adaptability, and fresh knowledge are at the heart of the finest CTE and middle-skill programs, marking a significant departure from old school vocational-ed programs.

National impacts
Political debates over inequality, fairness, minimum wages, free trade and global economics rage today. Helping ensure that more workers have the skills that employers and our marketplace need is not only the best route to the middle class for those individuals, but also the healthiest route to national success and happiness without resort to class conflicts, trade wars, national conflicts, forced wealth transfers, and government distortion of our economy.

Recent research by Nobel laureate Angus Deaton uncovered alarming life-span declines among white working-class Americans who have apparently been resorting to alcohol, drug addiction, and suicide at increased rates in response to economic disappointment—with the effects largely confined to those with a high-school education or less. Social reasons—the decline of marital stability, high out-of-wedlock births, sagging religious participation, and so forth—are probably involved in this as well. But a feeling of economic "dispossession" growing out of failures to participate successfully in our increasingly technological economy is undoubtedly involved, and are easier to reverse, through good technical education, than some of the social factors.

Stronger investments in CTE could also lower America's high drop-out rates for both high school and postsecondary education. U.S. Department of Education figures show that more than four out of ten students at four-year colleges, for instance, fail to graduate within six years. The career education programs profiled in this guidebook have far stronger completion rates, and keep engaged in schooling whole categories of students who would otherwise withdraw from education.

Career and technical education has the capacity to revolutionize both individual lives and our national economic soul. The purpose of this guidebook is to provide the best recipes for success. We will explore a host of approaches that donors are using. We'll extract the most useful nuggets on how to extend prosperity and improve our workforce, and use them to inform your own philanthropic giving. Whether you are a donor who has been active in field, or a newcomer, you'll learn lessons you can put to use immediately.

Linking Workers to the Skills Employers Need

Investments in postsecondary education are huge today. Federal, state, and local governments allocate tens of billions of dollars each year to subsidize institutions through Pell grants, federally-backed student loans, and direct payments to colleges and universities. Private philanthropy provided $38 billion in direct giving to higher education in 2014. There is, however, rising dissatisfaction with traditional college education. Here are some reasons why:

Rising costs

The price tag for four-year colleges and universities has risen much faster than inflation for years, making it the most rapidly inflating major sector of the economy. As a result, student debt has become a big problem. The heavy loans carried by the millennial generation (ages 16 to 34 as this book is written) are pushing up national default rates, and delaying marriage, childrearing, and the purchase of major assets such as homes and cars by young households.

Without quality gains

Soaring tuition prices have not produced corresponding rises in the quality of academic instruction. Most of the budgetary expansion has been administrative bloat and increased capital costs for construction and renovation, rather than for improved teaching.

High dropout rates

While almost 70 percent of high-school graduates enroll in college within two years of graduating, only 40 percent have obtained either an associate or bachelor's degree by their mid-20s. Just getting young people enrolled in college shouldn't be a priority, argues Drexel University economist Paul Harrington. Completing schooling with a credential is what produces a better economic life. "It's finishing college training that matters," he notes, and today's students and institutions are doing poorly on that front.

Degrees without obvious value

Even millennials who graduate are having trouble securing and maintaining employment. Many are overcredentialed for the jobs they accept. "This generation has been really cheated by having to take jobs in fields they're not trained for," states Bret Halverson, a member of the New York City Workforce Funders. "A college degree is not a career," notes Kent Misegades of the North Carolina Triangle Apprenticeship Program, an initiative profiled later in this guidebook. "It can be part of a career, but we tend to put the cart before the horse on that."

Skills mismatches with employers

Among "recent college graduates," report the authors of the labor study *Bridge the Gap,* "underemployment is rampant." "Too few have highly marketable skills; too many have pursued courses of study for which there is little demand."

"One of my favorite sayings is, 'Educated for what?'" says Mary "Penny" Enroth, president of the Palmer Foundation. "I think a lot of educators can't answer that question. They don't know the end goal."

Lack of practical skills
There is evidence that most employers now value practical work experience more highly than a high GPA or time at an elite college. A *Chronicle of Higher Education* analysis, for instance, showed that employers evaluating graduates for hiring gave more weight to internships, employment during college, college major, volunteer experience, and extracurricular activities than they did to GPA or college reputation. Yet conventional higher education pays scant attention to these sorts of practical experiences.

> The price tag on four-year colleges and universities is the most rapidly inflating sector of our economy.

Failure to keep pace with social change
Today's postsecondary student body includes rising percentages of working adults, who require schedule flexibility and convenient learning environments. It includes a growing proportion of first-generation college attendees coming out of weak public schools who need serious remedial help. It includes many students who want training in something other than liberal arts. "All available evidence suggests undergraduates simply aren't learning very much, even as they are being charged ever larger amounts of money and becoming increasingly burdened with debt," writes Kevin Carey in *The End of College*.

Training after high school is needed

Even as the return on investment at conventional colleges becomes dubious for many students, Americans who wish to succeed in our modern economy need training beyond high school. That remains an integral step to achieving a middle-class standard of living. The challenge is to create new forms of useful, cost-effective postsecondary education and credentialing.

Georgetown University's Center on Education and the Workforce recently reported that workers who gained comparatively quick and inexpensive practical credentials in high-demand technical fields outearned many counterparts with four-year degrees. Among young workers holding licenses and certificates, 43 percent out-earned holders of associate degrees, and 27 percent out-earned holders of bachelor's degrees.

While recipients of bachelor's degrees will still often have higher life-time earnings than those who obtain certifications or two-year degrees, these higher earnings never materialize if the student picks a field that is not in demand, or, worse, fails to complete a degree at all—as many millions of college entrants do today. Given the right opportunities and support, many of these failed four-year students could be trained in a career where they would be eminently useful, and personally successful.

One crucial aspect of effective career education is identifying the sectors of the regional economy that most need productive workers. This will vary somewhat across the country, so philanthropists and business leaders and local educators need to stay in close contact to monitor needs over time. But there are certain broad trends.

A recent McKinsey Global Institute report identified economic sectors where middle-skill jobs are likely to be in demand in many places. The industries included health care, IT and similar business services, leisure and hospitality, construction, and manufacturing. These areas plus retail jobs "account for 66 percent of employment today" and by 2020 will "account for up to 85 percent of new jobs created." Another analysis by the National Center for Career and Technical Education identified health care and hospitality as the two swiftest growing CTE career clusters. The same report found that STEM and IT jobs are paying the best wages.

More specific examples of jobs where employers report shortages of talented workers to the U.S. Bureau of Labor Statistics include these:

- Cybersecurity specialist, Web developer, graphic designer, architect, IT support associate, network administrator, paralegal.
- Registered nurse, lab and diagnostic technician, phlebotomist, medical coder, ultrasound tech, dental assistant, physical therapist assistant, physician assistant, biotechnology lab associate, personal care aide, home health aide, medical secretary, occupational therapy aide.
- Plumber, electrician, auto mechanic, welder, mechanical insulation worker, brick or stonemason, machinist, warehouse associate, woodworker, aircraft and avionics technician.

- Industrial engineering technician, robotics engineer, mechatronics engineer, electrical engineering technician, nuclear technician, aerospace engineer, petroleum technician, chemical technician.
- Air-traffic controller, shipping and receiving associate, fleet manager, cargo and freight agent, flight attendant.
- Equipment technicians and operators, irrigation engineer, soil scientist, surveyor.

Training workers for available jobs: A checklist

Recognizing that opportunities are plentiful for middle-skill jobs, how can philanthropists help match workers to these positions? The goal of this guidebook is to identify the most promising strategies to connect people with good positions in these booming fields. So we interviewed dozens of donors, experts, and practitioners and asked one central question—what attributes make a career and technical education program successful? The most common answers included the following attributes:

- Align the training to the specific job needs of high-demand industries operating nearby.
- Make sure the programs are flexible, responsive to changing labor markets, and constantly updated for new technology, learning, and practices.
- Provide many convenient ways, times, and places for students to enter training, and to sequence their collection of credentials.
- Closely integrate academic learning with technical skills and real-world job training.
- Provide direct routes from high school to training to employment.
- Ensure the teaching is good.
- Ensure the training and equipment are up-to-date.
- Ensure the curriculum is tied to the latest best practices and approaches.
- Confirm that students leave with all of the skills necessary to do a real job well.
- Offer built-in counseling and coaching, particularly during transition points, and help as much as possible with practical matters like transportation and child care.

- Provide stackable credentials that allow participants to accumulate skills gradually and sequentially, each building on past training and experience.
- Track graduates and make sure they get jobs, succeed in their first year, progress occupationally, and ultimately manage to support families on their wages.

Partnerships with nonprofits, schools, and businesses

In addition to identifying the middle-skill jobs most in demand in their region, and deciding what makes for an effective training approach, donors must find partners. The best career and technical education usually grows out of alliances among nonprofits, schools, and employers. Sometimes philanthropists will have to lead their partners from those other sectors.

At times, educators start out with objections to the idea of helping feed workers to for-profit companies. "The notion of becoming a 'supplier' may be alien or even objectionable to educators," notes Harvard University's *Bridge the Gap* report. In particular, warns Dennis Parker of Toyota's Advanced Manufacturing Program, it can be difficult to get academic institutions to understand one necessary perspective-shift behind effective CTE education: "The old customer was the student. The new customer is the employer."

Some academic institutions still have the perception that CTE programs are subpar, don't produce high-quality results, and consign students to the margins of the workforce. It's crucial to knock down these misperceptions, say Plinio Ayala, president of the New York City-based training nonprofit Per Scholas (profiled later in this guidebook). The best way to help academics get over these objections, the *Bridge the Gap* authors suggest, is to remind them that "providing a basis for the students they serve to achieve success in life" is the foremost task of any educator—and CTE education linked tightly to job markets is emphatically an excellent way to do that, particularly among at-risk students.

On the flip side, there are employers who will object to being asked to train the next generation of workers. Some feel they are under no obligation to build programs to develop the talents of a new generation of Americans—that's the job of education, they object, funded in part by their own corporate taxes. Still others are concerned that their competitors will siphon away the workers they train. Donors can help businesspeople move beyond this, into understanding of the enormous upside of having new streams of productive people flowing through their community.

The employer's alternative, writes Nancy Hoffman in *Schooling in the Workplace*, is the more-and-more ineffective old way: "Hire on the basis of level of schooling completed, major field of study, and personal characteristics, and then provide the job-specific training needed." A 2011 report by Harvard University's Graduate School of Education entitled *Pathways to Prosperity: Meeting the Challenge of Preparing Young Americans for the 21st Century* argued there is a smarter route:

> In recent years, [business leaders] have been at the forefront in championing such reforms as choice and accountability. But for the most part, they have left the job of educating and working with young adults to educators. True, they do provide extensive training to young adults once they have left school and been hired…. But the pathways system we envision would require them to become deeply engaged in multiple ways at an earlier stage—in helping to set standards and design programs of study; in advising young people; and most importantly, in providing greatly expanded opportunities for work-linked learning. In the process, employers would become full partners in the national effort to prepare young adults for success.

In a Harvard Business School report that came out three years later, researchers Michael Porter and Jan Rivkin further underscore the importance of employer involvement in education and training:

> We see a need for business leaders to act—to move from an opportunistic patchwork of projects toward strategic, collaborative efforts that make the average American productive enough to command higher wages even in competitive global labor markets. Without such actions, the U.S. economy will continue to do only half its job, with many citizens struggling. And in the long run, American business will suffer from an inadequate workforce, a population of depleted consumers, and large blocs of anti-business voters. Businesses cannot thrive for long while their communities languish.

Donors can become the catalyst for breaking down these barriers and expanding collaborations between nonprofits, schools, and for-profit employers. What's more, wise givers can make the difference that will help CTE and middle-skill training revolutionize the economy.

Philanthropists grab the flag of career and technical education

Helping lead and coordinate a national shift toward collaborative career and technical education is prime territory for philanthropists. In many places it is a task that will lack other natural advocates, because it falls between the stools of education and work, between the interests of the public sector and the private sector. And it is natural charitable work, in that it will bring benefits to individuals, communities, and nation alike.

"It's going to require a lot of money, but ultimately it will be less money than we spend to subsidize, feed, house, and incarcerate those who fall out of the traditional education structure," says David Fischer, a workforce-development expert at the Center for an Urban Future in New York City. In his 2015 book *America Needs Talent*, Lumina

> While almost 70 percent of high-school graduates enroll in college within two years of graduating, only 40 percent have obtained a degree by their mid-20s.

Foundation president Jamie Merisotis argues that philanthropists and others should push for a thoroughgoing reorientation of our system of higher education in order to make it serve the interests of students rather than the institutional needs of colleges and universities.

"We must ask ourselves what type of product we want to be sold and produced by the nation's colleges and universities and other providers of postsecondary learning," he urges. "In the ideal scenario…every student will know where he or she is going, how much it will cost to get there, how much time it will take, and what to expect at journey's end—both in terms of learning outcomes and career prospects." Very little of that is possible under today's reflex toward a state-college liberal-arts degree for all.

Thankfully, many enterprising donors and foundations—both large and small—are picking up a modernized vision of what postsecondary education should include. Merisotis' Indianapolis-based Lumina Foundation is one of the most influential examples. Lumina is using its endowment of more than a billion dollars to try to raise the percentage of Americans who have achieved a high-quality postsecondary degree or credential to 60 percent by 2025. The current figure is around 40 percent.

Lumina emphasizes the importance of a *high-quality* credential that provides practical knowledge and skills immediately applicable in the marketplace. In later chapters we'll further explore Lumina's leadership in this area. This includes through publications that spread information about the most promising models and examples of career and technical education.

Another philanthropy active in this area is the Bill & Melinda Gates Foundation. Gates has been beating the drum for some time now on the importance of postsecondary *success*, particularly for low-income enrollees. We must not get distracted by figures on college enrollment, Bill Gates himself has been urging, but always keep an eye on rates of completion of usable credentials and degrees. His foundation is working on different aspects of improving postsecondary outcomes, including expanding personalized learning. Creating better pathways to completion. Improving the reliability of completion data. Creating software that tracks student progress. Strengthening financial aid. And strengthening the public image of career and technical education, including by supporting organizations such as Jobs for the Future and the ACT Foundation.

Regional donors take the lead

Family philanthropies are also making a difference. One example is the Morgridge Family Foundation, which averages $10 million in annual giving. The foundation began in this area when Carrie Morgridge noticed that some low-income children in her community needed eyeglasses. From that humble beginning, the foundation now devotes nearly two thirds of its grantmaking to education and poverty-fighting organizations, many of them involved in vocational education and workforce development.

The Morgridge Family Foundation specializes in providing seed money to get initiatives off the ground and then stepping back so that support from other funders and self-sufficiency are pursued. "Every person we partner with knows they have a three-year runway and then we're out," says Carrie Morgridge. In addition to a rainbow of nonprofits, the foundation consistently funds community colleges and technical schools, viewing career education as the best pathway to success for many lower-income Americans. Foundation official John Farnam explains that they prioritized career and technical education after discovering that "getting kids to just finish high school or college is the wrong finish line. Providing opportunities for a family to earn a livable-wage job is the right goal."

Operating mainly through giving by her company and individual giving from her personal wealth, donor Karen Buchwald Wright has funded a network of technical and trades-oriented public colleges and training programs in central Ohio. Along with her four grown sons, Wright owns the Ariel Corporation, a leading manufacturer of gas compressors. Ariel's workforce offers a nearly perfect profile of the kind of middle-skill workers that are now crucial to our economy.

Wright has worked with area schools—including Stark State, Central Ohio Technical College, Zane State, and the Knox County Career Center—to develop curricula useful for technical education. One of her most significant gifts came when she donated $1 million to the Knox County Career Center to replace aging equipment in its machining lab. Through the nonprofit foundation she established in 2009, Wright has also funded engineering and nursing scholarships at Mount Vernon Nazarene University, and supported STEM efforts in the local public-school system, including a grant to a local high school for an engineering program.

Another notable example of local support for career and technical education is the Pinkerton Foundation. It provides $14 million of annual giving in the New York City area to support career internships, industry-specific certifications, and rigorous job training that teaches both hard (technical) skills and soft (social) skills needed to advance in the workplace. Focusing on at-risk youth, Pinkerton works closely with regional employers so that the right skillsets are provided and the right jobs are available to graduates. The foundation has made significant investments in nonprofits such as Jobs for the Future, Year Up, the Paraprofessional Healthcare Institute, and Stride for Success.

Also in New York City, foundations like Tiger, Achelis, Annie Casey, Clark, and JPMorgan Chase, and others have made important investments to build middle-skill for young adults through a nonprofit called JobsFirstNYC. Donors and businesses have also worked closely with some administrators within the New York City public schools who understand the importance of career and technical education. Creative approaches to supporting CTE took root during the Bloomberg administration. Some of these involve providing public-school students with opportunities to learn technical jobs within the film and video production industry, or to train in aviation mechanics at the New York airports.

Other foundations are making a difference in their home areas. The Claude Worthington Benedum Foundation is headquartered in Pittsburgh but serves southwestern Pennsylvania and the entire state of West Virginia. Funded by Michael Benedum, an early entrepreneur in the oil and gas business, the philanthropy makes $3 million of grants each year to CTE projects in K-12 schools and community colleges. About a decade ago the foundation decided to focus on reigniting its region's blue-collar workforce by building up valuable credentialing programs and associate degrees. Funding career academies within high schools, to integrate career-based training right into the core academic curriculum, has been one emphasis.

Across the country in Silicon Valley, the Sobrato Family Foundation has been another regional paragon for career and technical education.

> A college degree is not a career. It can be part of a career, but we tend to put the cart before the horse on that.

Real-estate mogul John Sobrato is supporting organizations that build ladders to middle-skill jobs for low-skilled workers in the San Francisco Bay Area. The need to qualify for higher-wage work is particularly acute in this region because it has one of the most expensive costs of living in the country, yet a third of local workers earn less than $18 per hour. Initiatives like Job Train, the Stride Center, the Bay Area chapter of Year Up, and training from the McKinsey Social Initiative have been recent targets of Sobrato family investments.

In the City of Brotherly Love, the Lenfest Foundation recently decided that instilling career-readiness skills in youths was one of the most significant ways it could improve the long-term health of the Philadelphia region. This foundation created by Gerry and Marguerite Lenfest out of their cable television fortune has so far been responsible for more than $1.2 billion in giving. The foundation is pursuing its latest goal through three related efforts—career and technical education, supporting industry-specific experiences for youths, and funding broad workforce development. It has invested in such nonprofits as YouthBuild Philadelphia, and Penn Medicine's medical internship program.

The family foundation established by Starbucks founder Howard Schultz announced in 2015 it was committing $30 million to workforce training for young people with support for many different nonprofits, training initiatives, and collaborations with employers. The Starbucks company also now offers, in collaboration with Arizona State University, a tuition reimbursement plan for all of its part- and full-time workers to help them acquire career training that will allow them to step beyond the coffee house to higher opportunities. Most of their employees say that is part of their eventual life plan after beginning at a lower-skill job with Starbucks.

Philanthropic-minded companies are also seeing the benefits of bridging the gaps that leave too many middle-skill jobs unfilled today. JPMorgan Chase has committed $250 million over five years to create career pathways nationally and internationally. Companies like IBM and Applied Software have created what they call "boot camps" where young computer programmers can build their skills and acquire credentials they can take to employers, without expensive or time-consuming formal education. Similar "competency-based" programs are being created across the country by a mix of businesses and educators.

A national vocational-ed effort which completely intermixes businesses and philanthropies is the recently launched 100,000 Opportunities Initiative. Companies like Alaska Airlines, Hilton, J. C. Penney, Macy's, Microsoft, Starbucks, Taco Bell, Target, and Walmart will provide jobs, internships, and apprenticeships to 100,000 young people over a three-year period. Donors such as the Schultz, Kellogg, JPMorgan Chase, Rockefeller, and Joyce foundations are providing crucial support to the effort. More on that in Chapter 4.

Many savvy observers within American philanthropy, business, and education are seeing the dire need today for more points of entry into career and technical education. In the next four chapters we'll explore more specific ways that donors can reach both young people about to enter the labor force and adults who are already working, to help them become as productive and successful as their energies allow.

Investing in Career and Technical Education in Secondary Schools

In today's comparatively weak job market, millennials in their teens and 20s faced an April 2016 youth unemployment rate of 11 percent. Others are not even looking for work, after becoming discouraged. As a double whammy, many of these young people are carrying heavy student-loan debts. Some young people are just idling in their parents' home; others are enrolling in college or graduate school as a way of delaying work until (they hope) the economy improves. Others cycle through low-paying service jobs with little chance of meaningful pay increases or advancement beyond low-skill jobs.

The declining economic power of the young is vividly seen in a recent Georgetown University report entitled *Failure to Launch: Structural Shift and the New Lost Generation.* "In 1980, young men earned 85 cents for each dollar of the average wage; by 2011, they earned only 58 cents on the dollar," write authors Anthony Carnevale, Andrew Hanson, and Artem Gulish. "In 1981, the wage gap between young and prime-age workers was $13,000; by 2008, the gap increased by 46 percent to $19,000."

When young people fall out of the work force, or fail to thrive when in it, there are ramifications far beyond economics. Those who are struggling for secure jobs tend to delay other major life decisions, like establishing their own household, marrying a spouse, having children. An estimated one fourth of 18- to 34-year olds still lived with their parents in 2015. Unprecedented in recent history, a solid portion of millennials are expected to remain unmarried until age 40.

Weak national economic trends are exacerbated by other factors that cast a pall over the job prospects of many youths coming out of high school and transitioning into adulthood. These include a mismatch between the skills and credentials employers need and what schools are teaching. Less early work experience by teenagers is also a factor, leaving young people less job-ready in many practical ways (soft skills and technical skills alike) when they do enter the workforce.

The good news is that career and technical education can directly address precisely these problems, and dramatically alter the trajectory of young people—especially young people who are exposed to good vocational training while they are still in high school, and forming their earliest attachments to work. "Those who find work early in young adulthood tend to stay in work going forward," notes David Fischer of the Center for an Urban Future. "When you give young people the opportunity, they can seize the moment. We need to give young people more moments to seize."

A 2016 report from the Thomas Fordham Institute did a careful academic study of high-school students to see whether those exposed to career and technical education (specifically, modern CTE courses closely aligned to current industrial needs) benefited or not. "Due to many decades of neglect and stigma…high-quality CTE is not a meaningful part of the high-school experience of millions of American students," the study noted. And "it's time to change that," according to author Shaun Dougherty of the University of Connecticut.

This conclusion flowed from three key findings of the study. Comparisons of students who had been exposed to CTE to those who hadn't showed the following:

- Students with greater exposure to CTE are more likely to graduate from high school, more likely to enroll in a two-year college, more likely to be employed, and more likely to earn higher wages.
- CTE is not a pathway away from college: Students taking more CTE classes are just as likely to pursue a four-year degree as their peers.
- CTE provides the greatest boost to kids who have been lagging most in recent years and need help—boys, and students from lower-income families.

Keith Leaphart, board chairman of the Lenfest Foundation in Philadelphia, has a personal connection to this topic. He credits early attachment to work for being the factor that saved his life as an inner-city youth. "The major difference between me and my friends—many of whom ended up in the criminal justice system or dead—was that I was able to get into work early," Leaphart says. "Instead of ending up as a drug dealer at 12-years-old, I ended up with a paper route."

Motivated by keystone research by labor economist Andrew Sum at Northeastern University, the Gap Foundation (funded by the clothing retail chain that includes Old Navy, Banana Republic, and Athleta) overhauled its giving strategy in 2006 to focus more acutely on creating job opportunities for teens. The impetus was the finding that early attachment to work yields many positive outcomes, while delays in working produce a domino effect of negative consequences. "If you get your first job at 25-years-old, versus 16- or 17-years-old, you're really in a catch-up mode for many, many years," states Gail Gershon of the Gap Foundation. As a result, the foundation shifted all of its youth-focused philanthropic funding into career readiness.

This chapter will explore avenues for giving young people valuable vocational experiences during their teenage schooling. The two chapters that follow expand on this by describing models of career and technical education created by for-profit corporations and nonprofit organizations, respectively. Each of these give donors many lessons to glean.

Donor investments in schools or students

Many public-school systems have elements of vocational ed in their curricula. The Denver Public Schools, for instance, offer CTE and STEM pathways in eight high schools. In North Carolina, the state public-school system includes a whole division for career and technical education. It supports and oversees CTE credentialing across the state.

The New York City Public Schools became a model during the Bloomberg and Giuliani administrations for integrating good vocational training into high schools. "Some 50 of the city's roughly 400 high schools are dedicated exclusively to CTE," reports the Manhattan Institute. And nearly 75 other New York City public high schools run vocational ed programs (220 of them), where students can take vocational subject instruction. Overall, "some 40 percent of New York City teens take at least one CTE course while in high school; nearly 10 percent attend a dedicated CTE school."

> There is a mismatch between what high-school graduates bring to job sites, and what firms need.

The IBM Corporation has supported some very innovative high-level tech training in New York school. Their program Pathways in Technology Early College High School, known as P-TECH, fully integrates technical training into a traditional school structure by blending four years of high school with two years of college. Although piloted in New York City, the P-TECH model has spread elsewhere. In addition to producing excellent technologists the approach appeals to some philanthropists because it mostly attracts minority students who are significantly under-represented in technology fields.

Some philanthropies take a simpler route and choose to undergird vocational education simply by offering relevant scholarships to high-school students as they transition to the next phase of their education. One fine example is the Daniels Fund, based in Denver. The late cable-television pioneer Bill Daniels created a major scholarship problem that helps hundreds of students every year as they graduate from high schools in Colorado, New Mexico, Utah, and Wyoming. In 2013, the fund decided to incorporate career elements into an effort that until then had been dominated by assumptions that students would enter traditional college tracks. The foundation now provides information about alternative jobs, what they pay, and the competencies and training needed to secure them.

A Daniels scholarship offers unique benefits to students. Each recipient works with mentors to develop a graduation plan, plotting the sequence of courses needed to enter a chosen career path. There is a strong element of accountability in the scholarship. If students fail to meet their end of the responsibilities, they have to pay for that particular semester out of pocket. Yet there are also second chances: Students can reapply for the scholarship.

The Daniels Fund has also established relationships with employers in their four-state coverage area to determine the regional workforce needs. In addition to having access to various forms of technical training that will be valuable in the workforce, scholarship awardees get training in the social job skills. They watch 32 videos on soft-skill development, and participate in a four-day orientation which includes etiquette training, instruction on how to make small talk, and insights on how to pursue true success in life.

Project Lead The Way
One of the easiest and most effective ways for funders to begin supporting career and technical education in public schools is to support Project Lead The Way. This philanthropy-driven nonprofit has become the nation's most successful provider of science, technology, engineering, and mathematics instruction for K-12 students. It began in upstate New York in 1986, where public high-school teacher Richard Blais wanted to encourage more of his students to study engineering. Within a few years, Blais was not only attracting lots of kids to his hands-on classes in digital electronics and other subjects, but leaving them with valuable skills important in technology occupations. With early funding from the Charitable Leadership Foundation, PTLW was launched in 1997 across a network of 12 New York school districts. The next year two New Hampshire schools joined. The first major corporate sponsor signed on in 1999, when Autodesk began to provide students with its world-leading computer-assisted-design software.

The program—which combines college-level technology concepts with exciting project-based learning (building and then racing a solar-powered car, creating fighting robots, using laser machine tools and print-jet manufacturing)—proceeded to grow explosively. By 2008, PLTW was being used in schools in all 50 states. The Kern Family Foundation gave the organization a $10 million gift in 2009 to allow further major expansion, and donated a total of more than $26 million over the next several years. In 2013, Chevron made a $6 million donation. The program's many other donors include the Kauffman, Knight, and Conrad foundations, and companies like Lockheed Martin.

At a time when the U.S. has a million unfilled technology jobs, engineering colleges, other educators, and employers have come to prize alumni from the PLTW courses—who score higher on math and tech tests, say they want to study engineering or computer science or other tech-related fields in seven cases out of ten, and drop out of university engineering programs at just one quarter the national rate of attrition. Clarkson University was one of the first high-quality tech schools to offer scholarships directly to PLTW students, and at some engineering schools today between 40 and 60 percent of the freshmen enrolled are alums of the project. Toyota and other employers also now fast-track PLTW graduates into their technical training programs and skilled jobs.

In 2015, more than 8,000 schools (now not only high schools but also middle and elementary campuses) used PLTW curricula. In this way, Project Lead The Way exposed 900,000 students to high-quality technical education. Donors interested in investing in great vocational education at the K–12 level have a ready-made option in funding this nonprofit.

Philanthropies go deep in their home regions
In the sections that follow we will sketch other examples of philanthropic investments in CTE through school systems. In most of these cases the donors made an extended commitment to their region, and ultimately reaped strong results.

The Hendricks Family Foundation and Beloit schools
In Beloit, Wisconsin, a local donor is making investments to bootstrap a successful career academy that's located in a public school with many students from poor families. Beloit is a small manufacturing town where employers have solid trades-oriented jobs that they can't fill with local applicants, due to lack of middle-level skills. Philanthropist and

businesswoman Diane Hendricks aims to help students and companies alike with her initiative.

With a population of 37,000 people, Beloit suffered a stinging blow when advanced manufacturer Beloit Corporation declared bankruptcy in 2000 after nearly 150 years in business. In addition to economic woes, racial tensions have flooded the town. Gripped by race riots during the Rodney King era, Beloit was for a period known for having one of the highest per capita crime rates in the nation. Into this challenging atmosphere stepped Hendricks—chairman of Hendricks Holding Company, president of the Hendricks Family Foundation, and ranked by *Forbes* as the second most successful self-made woman in the U.S., commanding a net worth of over $4 billion.

Hendricks is aiming for both economic and social revivals in her hometown by making investments in career and technical education. One of her springboards has been Beloit Memorial High School, a large institution with a student population that is about three quarters Hispanic or black, and mostly low income.

> An associate degree is the gateway to a livable wage, to a career that has options for promotion and advancement over the years.

Like many other areas of the country, Beloit has been experiencing a paradox. Many young people and low-skill adults say they find it difficult to get jobs. Yet employers reported difficulty finding the workers they need. "We're in a geographic location where unemployment is high, yet local companies have an enormous need for qualified workers," says Kim Bliss of the Hendricks Family Foundation. The explanation for that gap is skills. There is a mismatch between what high-school graduates bring to job sites and what firms need. The Hendricks effort on vocational education is intended both to make sure that the things students learn are capabilities that employers value, and also to give fresh motivation to students to strive—by showing them that what they are asked to do in high school will help them build a better life once they're on their own. "Our goal is to help young people see education not just as preparation for college, but preparation for life," says Bliss.

Hendricks drew inspiration for her career center from a leading vocational ed program located near Allentown, Pennsylvania. The Lehigh Career & Technical Institute is one of the largest such organizations in the country, serving ten public high schools. Its well-regarded offerings include more than 50 programs, in areas ranging from commercial art to various electronic technologies, from cabinetmaking to health professions, from greenhouse management to machine tooling. The programs mix intensive hands-on instruction with solid academic work, and are structured to make sure graduates meet national skill standards established by industry leaders.

With a startup grant from Hendricks, BMHS set up a career academy oriented around manufacturing, technology, and the sciences. Key career pathways offered there include computer programming, advanced welding certifications, computer numerical control machining, construction and woodworking, auto mechanics, and engineering (through Project Lead The Way). Numerous apprenticeships are offered in local businesses. The career academy hosts monthly career panels for students, offers intervention services for troubled students, job recruitment fairs, and placement help for further study at community colleges.

Although still in its infancy, this program is an ambitious example of how an energetic donor can connect local high-school students with real jobs and postsecondary opportunities that lead to satisfying careers. And the investment was not huge. The Hendricks Family Foundation sparked this effort with a $300,000 spread over three years.

Bader Philanthropies and high-tech manufacturing
Elsewhere in Wisconsin, Bader Philanthropies has also created an inventive approach to vocational-technical education. As an umbrella organization for two foundations—the Helen Daniels Bader Fund and the Isabel and Alfred Bader Fund—Bader Philanthropies has awarded over $30 million in grants specifically targeted to workforce development over the last 25 years. Bader focuses on the Milwaukee area, and is particularly interested in creating work opportunities for minority and low-income populations.

In hope of broadening the economic horizons of soon-to-graduate students in Milwaukee, Bader was first drawn in 2013 to an ambitious school-to-work collaborative known as GPS Education Partners. The nonprofit helps school districts throughout Wisconsin plan, build, and operate education centers that recreate the manufacturing environments of local businesses. GPS Education Centers are staffed by state-certified teachers, and give students a realistic glimpse of what a successful career in modern manufacturing requires and offers.

Beginning in their junior year, participating high-school students experience a combination of hands-on manufacturing experience and academic instruction. They spend two hours every day in classrooms learning math, science, social studies, and practical life skills such as financial literacy. They also get instruction in technical subjects like blueprint reading, computer-aided design, and high-performance manufacturing. Students hone and practice this knowledge through six hours a day of practical, hands-on experience in the real work environment of an allied employer.

The program requires two consecutive years without a summer vacation, a full 24 months. That allows students to graduate not only with a high-school diploma but also with a head start on industry-recognized stackable credentials, transferable credits to postsecondary institutions, and an impressive track record of real work. GPS Education Partners is a rigorous example of how schools, businesses, and philanthropists can collaborate and merge operations to benefit students.

Bader Philanthropies has made several successive grants of $50,000 to a GPS center in Milwaukee as contributions to the effort. Bader has also challenged GPS to increase the financial commitments of employer partners. "The biggest challenges are how the employer community thinks about their own investment in the workforce, the talent pipeline, and what they need to contribute to make the partnerships a success in the long haul," says Bader's Jerry Roberts.

The Benedum Foundation helps schools teach engineering

The Claude Worthington Benedum Foundation is another donor that has had success in bringing career education to public schools. The foundation decided back in 2005 to make technical education a big part of its future work. This made geographic and demographic sense, because a majority of the jobs in the rural parts of Pennsylvania and West Virginia that fall under the Benedum Foundation's area of interest are blue-collar careers or ones that require an associate degree or certification.

"We very much wanted to emphasize the fact that an associate degree is the gateway to a livable wage, to a career that has options for promotion and advancement over the years," says James Denova, vice president of the foundation, in explaining the philanthropy's decision.

To mitigate the segregation caused by sending some students to college preparatory schools and others to vocationally oriented schools, the Benedum Foundation prioritizes investments in career academies embedded within public schools. A major benefit is that students needn't split their day between two different institutions, one academically oriented and the other offering job training; both aspects are housed under one roof.

One example funded by the Benedum Foundation is located in the Chartiers Valley School District of southwestern Pennsylvania. With Benedum support, Chartiers added an advanced-manufacturing academy to its high school, where students can earn up to 30 college credit hours and certificates in manufacturing and fabrication through Project Lead The Way. In this program, students bound for a four-year college work right alongside those headed to community college. "The career academies function as majors for high-school students, in much the same way that professional schools function in higher education," Denova explains.

Impressed by the success of this manufacturing academy, the Benedum Foundation offered Chartiers Valley grants totaling $403,000 to allow the school district to become a national training center for Project Lead The Way. This will enable 25 other schools to get their teachers trained at Chartiers Valley so they can set up their own Project Lead The Way programs. Part of this process involves a partnership with the West Virginia University College of Engineering, which now confers college credits to Chartiers Valley high-school students.

Benedum's investment was seconded by $375,000 of philanthropic support from the Chevron Corporation. Benedum focused on paying for the training center coordinator, professional development for teachers, and outreach. Chevron provided money to individual schools in Pennsylvania, Ohio, and West Virginia so they could purchase equipment and build their own Project Lead The Way programs. The pleasing result is a regional consortium that is bringing Project Lead The Way's excellent, proven technical education to thousands of students across a three-state region.

Health-care career academies from the Claude Moore Foundation
In 2007, the Claude Moore Charitable Foundation forged a relationship with Loudoun County High School in northern Virginia. Together, they created a health-care academy embedded in the school. The academy trains students in practical nursing, medical lab technology, pharmacy

careers, radiology, surgical sterilization, dentistry, medical information, EMT response, and other areas. Students can dual enroll in many of these fields at Northern Virginia Community College while they are still in high school. Some tracks allow students to begin introductory courses in medicine starting in their sophomore year, then select specific medical career tracks in their junior and senior years, and then move directly from high school to a job at INOVA Hospital.

The foundation has already expanded its health career academy model to three other school districts—in Frederick County, Maryland, and in the northern Virginia cities of Winchester and Alexandria. It is studying further expansion, most immediately in Fairfax County and a higher-poverty area of Roanoke. So far, the Moore Foundation has devoted $3.5 million to establishing these health-care career academies, and produced more than 600 graduates.

"One of the key features of the program is that kids receive dual enrollment credit with whatever community college we happen to partner with in that jurisdiction," says Lynn Tadlock of Moore. "The tuition costs are paid by the program, so basically, they have almost a semester's worth of college credit at no charge to them." Foundation director J. Lambert suggests that "if we can help these young people make a good living and obtain self-sufficiency, without having to go to four or six years of college, we've beaten the game."

The Bean Foundation helps mix in creativity and communication
Some funders have tried to combine technical training with the classic benefits of liberal arts instruction. Beginning in 2014, the New Hampshire-based Norwin and Elizabeth Bean Foundation poured energy into an ambitious collaboration at Manchester High School West known as STEAM Ahead (standing for science, technology, engineering, arts, and math). This high school lost many of its college-track students when a nearby town decided to build its own high school. New leaders then decided to make high-quality vocational training a distinctive offering of Manchester West.

The initiative's published list of "aspirations" explain its unique positioning: "New Hampshire needs more graduates with skill and knowledge in science, technology, engineering," starts the mission statement. Yet "the arts and humanities capture...what it means to create." So this program's "push for twenty-first century skills includes not only innovation and technology but also creativity, collaboration, and communication."

The initiative links the high school with Manchester Community College and several campuses of the university system of New Hampshire. This allows students to earn credit for a full year of college classes while they receive firsthand job experience. Their jobs are at local industry partners SilverTech and Dyn, or other firms, and sometimes result in a schedule which has high-school juniors and seniors in the school three days per week and on the job two days per week.

The Bean Foundation started its support with an initial grant of $25,000 in 2014. It next offered that much more as a matching grant if the high school could secure additional funding. SilverTech stepped up, bringing the total gifts to $75,000. Technology firm Dyn, hoping it would eventually be able to hire graduates of the program, later donated $150,000. The pilot effort began with 60 students and has since expanded.

"The project answered a need in the school. It has sound leadership. And it's an impressive collaboration among a range of stakeholders," summarizes Kathy Cook of the Bean Foundation.

> It's a trade, entrepreneurship, civics, and character-education program all rolled into one three-year period.

The Irvine Foundation and Linked Learning

The San Francisco-based James Irvine Foundation has created a program in California known as Linked Learning. Designed to ignite the career ambitions of high-school students, it mixes academic instruction with vocational and real-world job experience through job shadowing, apprenticeships, internships, and other opportunities. The effort also includes supports and services to ensure that students stay on course and graduate.

The project grew out of an effort to improve schooling completion rates for low-income Californians age 16 to 24. Foundation staff quickly saw that mixing college prep training with career training in high schools would be essential to success in this. So they explored a number of models across the country that attempted this, and then created their own marriage of academics and vocational prep.

"It answered the question for these high-school students about why these classes mattered. And how they would lead to a family-sustaining wage and a real job, not just to a four-year college—which, for many of them, was modeled nowhere in their environment," says Daniel Silverman of the Irvine Foundation.

Irvine piloted its new program in nine California school districts. The foundation also had to get involved in public relations and public-policy advocacy, because existing state policies mandated that students spend precisely determined amounts of time in the classroom. This would have prevented the out-of-classroom career training at the heart of Linked Learning from being possible, and had to be overturned.

Perhaps the greatest testament to Linked Learning's success is how it has attracted alternative funding sources.

From 2006 to 2015, the Irvine Foundation invested more than $100 million into Linked Learning—making it one of the foundation's largest efforts. One indicator of its success is that the program has grown to the point that the state of California has now committed $2 billion to support its obligations to running the initiative in public schools. The model has also spread to other states. Ford Foundation funds brought Linked Learning to Detroit, Houston, and other regions. The National Academy Foundation is also bringing it to bear elsewhere.

Linked Learning has produced some impressive results. Participating high-school students completed more classes and had a lower dropout rate and higher graduation levels than counterparts on a conventional academic track. Seven percent more high-school students went on to postsecondary education. And the students who attended the career academies earned an average of $10,000 more in the four years following high school. A total of 18,200 California high-school students were enrolled in 2015.

Linked Learning is continuing to expand. In collaboration with public schools and community colleges, the Irvine Foundation is providing funding to bring the initiative to 63 new districts across the Golden State. The secret to Irvine's success, according to Silverman, is that Linked Learning is able to convince low-income youth that the academic and career work it asks of them will directly and immediately help them in finding good work. This excites passion in the students. "It's academic coursework done in the context of career," he summarizes.

Charter schools make CTE a specialty: The cases of SIATech and YouthBuild Philadelphia

While career and technical education is becoming an element in traditional public schools in more and more cases, it is in charter schools where career-preparedness has often become a full-blown specialty. And because they lack the bureaucratic layers of conventional public education, making the process of creating programs and enacting change far easier, charter schools can be particularly enticing for donor investments. In addition, many charter schools are already focused on reaching at-risk students, so offering workforce training within their halls is often a winning approach for multiple parties.

One high-profile national model for charter-school success in this area is the School for Integrated Academics and Technologies, or SIATech. It operates charter schools in California, Arkansas, Arizona, Florida, and New Mexico that are specifically organized to transform high-school dropouts into useful employees. Each campus adjoins a Jobs Corps center administering a federal program that offers occupational training for high-school dropouts.

Through an effective mix of online and in-person instruction, SIATech helps dropouts earn a full high-school diploma instead of a GED. The average student enrolled in their program makes two years' worth of academic gains in literacy and math in just one year's time. This academic work is matched with technical training at the Jobs Corps site. With this combination of instruction, graduates emerge with much improved employability.

On a more local level, YouthBuild Charter School of Philadelphia is an instructive model because of its scope, ambition, and fearlessness. One of approximately 226 chapters of the national YouthBuild USA, a nonprofit devoted to helping low-income youths between the ages of 18 and 21 become productive adults, this school offers equal parts academic instruction and real-world job training. Its features four career tracks: building trades and construction, health care, childcare services, and customer service.

Students come from at-risk populations, including those who are aging out of foster care, are single parents, struggle with homelessness, and those with a criminal record. Fully 100 percent of YouthBuild Philadelphia's students are high-school dropouts. Left to their own devices, most of these young people would remain on the economic sidelines—or worse. But this charter school opens healthy possibilities through a powerful mixture of learning and work.

Founded in 1991 and awarded charter-school status in 1997, YouthBuild Philadelphia now offers a 12- to 15-month program split between competency-based academics that lead to a high-school diploma, and hands-on job training. Mixed in is a foundation of support services that help young people stay on track, plus a community-service pathway (in partnership with AmeriCorps) that helps students develop a pro-social ethic.

The school serves around 200 students annually. Incoming learners are divided into two groups that alternate six-week sessions in the classroom and workplace. After they graduate, some transition immediately to full-time jobs, others pursue postsecondary training. A strong emphasis on dual enrollment and bridge programming helps the students who want to go on to community college or college make that transition.

Work experience runs the gamut. Through the school's most traditional track, construction, students rebuild and refurbish abandoned houses. They learn the technical side of the business—blueprint reading and cost-estimating—in addition to the manual tasks of masonry, framing, door and window installation, and interior finishing. The pathway culminates in an industry-recognized credential from the National Center for Construction Education and Research.

Community colleges are "one of the best anti-poverty programs in the U.S."

Another track, health care, provides certification and training in nurse-aide skills through service at nursing homes, ultimately leading to a home health aide or certified nursing assistant credential. The school has also developed a child development associate track. Students put in volunteer hours at daycare centers, and once they have graduated have many entry points into the local workforce, which is short of qualified workers amid the growth of pre-K education in Philadelphia.

Recently, YouthBuild Philadelphia revamped its IT and business administration track. School administrators recognized a growing need for customer service employees in Philadelphia businesses. In a partnership with Starbucks Corporation, the school now guides students into paid jobs at local coffeehouses that also provide pathways into postsecondary education.

To supplement its academics and workforce training, YouthBuild Philadelphia provides each student with case-management services, plus a staff mentor. This helps with the school's emphasis on developing soft skills. "We are unapologetically comprehensive," says Simran Sidhu,

YouthBuild Philadelphia's executive director. "We relentlessly change and adapt depending on what students need to get where they need to go."

Another of the school's key markers is a close working relationship with local employers. Each training track has an advisory board where community business leaders offer input on best practices and changes and updates that may be needed. The school is now exploring new ways of keeping in touch with students after they graduate, to ensure they remain on track. Mechanisms include regular care packages, and monthly offers of transportation passes to make remaining in college easier.

In addition to the public funds it receives as a charter school, Youth-Build Philadelphia has benefited strongly from private philanthropy. Donors fund many of its more innovative services. Local private funders include the Lenfest, JPMorgan Chase, Spruce, Claneil, Gates, Mott, and Walmart foundations. In an interview with us, Lenfest Foundation executive director Stacy Holland said she has never seen a youth-oriented organization better connect at-risk youth with job skills in so short a period of time. "They really do bring out the best in these young people," she observed.

Although these two examples primarily focus on at-risk youths, many more traditional charter schools also excel in career and technical training. For more examples from around the country, and covering many different populations, see The Philanthropy Roundtable's 2014 guidebook *From Promising to Proven: A Wise Giver's Guide to Expanding on the Success of Charter Schools.*

Robert Luddy brings CTE to low-cost private schools, and American apprenticeships

Funders can extract many recipes for success from the example of North Carolina businessman, entrepreneur, and philanthropist Robert Luddy in bringing career and technical education to private schools. More than a decade ago Luddy faced a quandary after successfully launching a Catholic school (St. Thomas More Academy) and high-achievement charter school (Franklin Academy) in North Carolina's tech-saturated Research Triangle Park. Franklin Academy's success as a public charter school had led to long waiting lines of parents coveting a spot for their child. But a state-imposed cap on the creation of new charters blocked Luddy from meeting the demand by launching fresh schools. So this analytical engineer took an inventive approach.

Luddy launched a network of nonprofit, low-cost private elementary, middle, and high schools called Thales Academy. These could serve the rapidly growing population of families in Wake County looking for educational standards without prohibitive tuition costs. The idea was a success from the start, and families have eagerly flocked to the schools in the ensuing years.

Thales Academy boasts a number of novel elements, including classical instruction, budget-friendly tuition ($5,300 per year for grades K-5, $6,000 per year for grades 6-12, with scholarships available for needy students), and a revenue model that relies exclusively on tuition, not taxpayer or continuing philanthropic support. Today, Thales is the largest network of private schools in North Carolina, with five campuses in Wake County.

Another place Luddy innovated is in technical education. Luddy is owner of a major manufacturing operation, the leading national kitchen-ventilation supplier CaptiveAire Systems. He both has a rich scientific background and recognizes the importance of job-readiness skills. So he created an optional STEM-intensive course of study at Thales's high schools. Known as the Luddy Institute of Technology, this track uses a special four-year curriculum throughout high school, and many enrolled students devote the summer between their junior and senior years to an industrial internship. From the outset, students are immersed in the fundamentals of engineering: traditional drafting techniques, then computer-aided design through SolidWorks. The basics of mechanisms, energy, statics, materials, and kinematics. The history of engineering and manufacturing. Automation, computer modeling, robotics, and flexible manufacturing systems.

One testament to the program's effectiveness is the demonstrated market value of its engineering training. In an interview with us, Luddy proudly pointed out that second-year students in the Luddy Institute of Technology track complete a certificate in SolidWorks, which alone would enable them to command between $40,000 and $60,000 as employees. "They're sophomores in high school, and they've already got these really extraordinary skills," he noted.

During their senior year, students complete either a capstone engineering design project or enroll in an apprenticeship. Upon graduating, students are well prepared for either a college track leading to a bachelor's degree in engineering from a four-year institution, or an apprenticeship in a middle-skill job.

Students who choose the apprenticeship path have another option supported by Luddy: the North Carolina Triangle Apprenticeship Program (NCTAP), a program adopted from Charlotte, North Carolina's Apprenticeship 2000 program. NCTAP is a rigorous 8,000-hour pathway that offers four years of on-the-job work experience, a consistent paycheck beginning in high school, and guaranteed job placement upon completion. The approach is modeled after the Swiss vocational-technical programs, which offer very flexible routes, ranging from apprenticeships through advanced degrees, into high-level technical careers.

NCTAP slots are not solely for Thales students. Instead, high-performing sophomores are recruited from numerous public, private, and home schools. The selection process for students is rigorous, and takes around ten months. The program has generating ample interest because the outcomes are enticing: a guaranteed job, a journeyman's certificate, and an associate degree in mechatronics from Wake Technical Community College. And since their college work is entirely paid by an employer, students leave the program with no student loan obligations and several years of salary behind them.

NCTAP relies on support from participating companies. Administrative costs are low; the most significant expense is the total $140,000 cost for each candidate, which the hiring company covers. That includes the expenses of community college tuition and the student's salary and benefits over four years. Given this sizable cost, each employer has plenty of skin in the game, and works hard to cultivate the student as a long-term employee. "Our partners want these young people to stay there for their whole careers," says former engineer Kent Misegades of NCTAP. "If they're good, they can go all the way to the top of those corporations with no more than a high-school diploma, apprenticeship, and associate degree."

On average, NCTAP makes around ten placements per year. It hopes to steadily increase that number every year. The program currently has nine corporate partners, including Luddy's CaptiveAire and the pharmaceutical giant GlaxoSmithKline. With its first class just starting in 2014, NCTAP is still in its infancy. It appears to hold immense promise, however. Matched with the right donors, the program is quite replicable in other places.

Career Cruising software

One practical way donors can help high schools and middle schools to the career education well is to buy them the software that helps students find job niches where they could thrive. There is a powerful tool available today and used by many schools and nonprofits. It's called Career Cruising, and with a subscription, teachers, administrators, nonprofit staff, and students can access it from anywhere an Internet connection is available.

Students use the software for a multi-step self-assessment process. The "Matchmaker" questionnaire leads students toward various occupational profiles, and helps them create plans to get there. They can also access a treasure trove of career-building aids, including current lists of available jobs in different fields (located by zip code), the range of likely wages, college and vocational programs required for a given vocation, scholarship opportunities, and best high-school classes to take in order to prepare. Career Cruising also has an integrated easily searchable database of internships and apprenticeships. There are even opportunities to interview existing workers in a field via the Internet.

The software is a powerful way to get young people thinking about the connections between what they are learning academically and what they will do vocationally. After using these assessment tools, learners have the option of creating an individualized career plan tailored to a chosen field. Teachers and administrators can track the progress of every student on completing his own assessment and plan.

Businessman and philanthropist Blouke Carus of the Carus Corporation has purchased Career Cruising software for organizations across his home Illinois Valley region. He funds a locally tailored version of the Career Cruising software at Illinois Valley Community College to provide easy access to local internship and job opportunities.

"There is a real need for a vehicle, like Career Cruising, to communicate between companies and schools," Carus says. "It opens opportunities for students to connect directly with employers, so young people aren't just cutting grass or flipping hamburgers in their early jobs, but doing something that reinforces their education."

Carus suggests Career Cruising software as a good beginning investment for donors. Funders can get the platform launched by paying for the licensing up front. And they can be especially helpful in convincing regional industries to enhance the offerings by posting local job information.

The software is available in both English and Spanish. With a donation from the Deutsche Bank Americas Foundation, the Bronx nonprofit Opportunities for a Better Tomorrow (profiled later in this book) has acquired the software so Spanish-speaking parents can use it to inform their kids about college options. This is the kind of practical tool that can open up many secondary opportunities for getting young people without a clear occupational focus to set themselves on a path to accomplishment.

Character also counts: The need to ensure a rounded education

While maintaining an essential focus on technical instruction, the finest examples of CTE programs still offer soft-skills learning—the warp and woof of how to perform and behave on the job—as a highly necessary ingredient in their formulas for success. Particularly among at-risk youths who emerge from unstable families, a vital first step amid vocational learning is formation of character. Honesty, timeliness, reliability, empathy for others—without these, career skills can be useless because the student will find it impossible to get others to work with him or her.

> You see how if you take the entry-level job, then earn additional credentials and certifications, you can move up the ladder.

To close out this chapter on vocational investments at the secondary-school level, we will profile one historic trade school that does a particularly superb job at weaving essential character education into the technical skill building it provides to its students: the Williamson College of the Trades. Based in an eastern suburb of Philadelphia, philanthropically created WCT has a mission of helping imperiled young men from underprivileged backgrounds equip themselves for a career in the trades that will both be profitable and allow them to live as men of honor. In addition to its academics and career training, Williamson puts an intense focus on faith, integrity, diligence, excellence, and service, aspiring to produce good citizens as well as good workers.

Thanks to its philanthropic endowment, Williamson is the only trades college in the U.S. to provides its students with full scholarships covering tuition, room and board, textbooks, and some personal expenses. It has a special orientation toward students of little financial means. Students apply to the program between their junior and senior year in high school.

It then provides them an additional three years of training. Enrollees can select from a wide variety of trades—like carpentry, masonry, horticulture, and machine-tool technology.

A three-year study conducted by Tufts University researchers compared the character development of youths at WCT with the progress of comparable young men at nearby schools in the Philadelphia area. Williamson students scored higher on the virtues of diligence, gratitude, honesty, love, reliability, thrift, hopeful future expectations, integrity, and faith when stacked against comparison students. They were also better engaged cognitively, emotionally, and behaviorally, and expressed feelings of being better prepared for their careers.

Dr. Richard Lerner and his academic team at Tufts conducted this research at the behest of the late philanthropist Jack Templeton. The John Templeton Foundation wanted to investigate whether WCT's emphasis on character played any significant role in the school's success at guiding at-risk men into useful lives. The results indicate that character-building education does yield many positive outcomes, and that other schools working with at-risk students and lacking this same focus might do well to add character formation to their curricula.

Lerner and his team were able to track Williamson alums back five decades. "These people not only became successful businessmen," he told us, "they became entrepreneurs and pillars of the community. So what this school offers is unique in our experience. It's a trade education. It's an entrepreneurship education. It's a civic education. And it's a character-education program, all rolled across one three-year period."

In 2008, the Williamson School received two large gifts. Henry Rowan donated $25 million, and Gerry Lenfest added another $20 million. These pledges buoyed the endowment that makes it possible for the institution to provide full scholarships.

Lenfest told *Philanthropy* magazine that "I feel there's been an overemphasis on college education. Vocational training has been neglected, but it makes sense for a lot of students." Rowan stated that "the lack of skills is very severe in the USA. You can't hire top-skilled individuals in machining and welding and in any of the trades. There's a terrible shortage of skilled people."

Lenfest added that in addition to its technical instruction, he was drawn to Williamson's emphasis on character. "Underneath it all, there is a moral and spiritual element to the education. It's a very powerful combination. The students there are not just learning a trade. They're learning to be good citizens. I would love to see Williamson replicated across the country. These young men learn about life. They leave the school prepared to be good workers, good husbands, and good fathers. They are ready to be responsible citizens in their communities. The country needs more of it."

School founder Isaiah Williamson was a devout Quaker, and WCT retains an active Christian approach. An important piece of its success formula is helping students think of vocation as more than a career and helping them see work as a form of service to God and fellow men, concepts recently explored by Tim Clydesdale in his book *The Purposeful Graduate: Why Colleges Must Talk to Students About Vocation.* Clydesdale calls for a new paradigm in higher education that engages students in meaningful conversations about calling and purpose in their lives—not just jobs. As they impart essential technical skills, excellent career and technical educators can also encourage this type of thinking, and help equip students to be responsible as well as competent—because we know that stellar, self-supporting workers and conscientious citizens are both of those things. This is ideal territory for robust philanthropic action.

Enlarging Employer-sponsored Pipelines

As vocational education continues its rebirth in the twenty-first century economy, many employers are opening their eyes to the value and necessity of creating their own youth-focused pipelines of talent. Sometimes they build these in-house, sometimes through intermediaries, and sometimes through cross-sector collaborations. Usually these are a mix of self-interest and philanthropy. There are many outstanding models to choose from.

In the past decade, several impressive national initiatives have arisen with strong financial backing from businesses. These include JPMorgan Chase's New Skills at Work and McKinsey's Generation USA programs. Although relatively young, such initiatives are already making inroads in bridging employment gaps among the young.

In other instances employers are creating workforce training right within their for-profit mission. Companies such as Toyota and Southwire have made generalized training for the next generation of workers a regular part of their business structures. Others, such as Norton Healthcare, profiled in Chapter 7, have strong programs for training their incumbent workers to move up from lower-level to higher-skill positions.

It can sometimes be difficult for donors to see a clear way to invest in these kinds of ventures alongside for-profit businesses. The options, however, are many. For instance, donors might pay for structural supports for a for-profit venture, such as the Career Cruising software profiled in Chapter 5 that connects young people with job opportunities. Or fund a media campaign to publicize tech and manufacturing careers, funneling interested parties to a business-organized training effort. There are many other possibilities. Besides, corporate initiatives seldom exist in isolation, and none of the finest examples operate solo. They commonly work closely with intermediaries like nonprofits, schools, local agencies, and community groups. This offers numerous points of entry for wise and eager philanthropists.

Large corporate initiatives

Following are five corporate initiatives that are wide in scope and ambition: 100,000 Opportunities, LeadersUp, Generation USA, New Skills at Work, and Grads of Life.

100,000 Opportunities and LeadersUp

Launched in August 2015, the 100,000 Opportunities Initiative is a collaboration of employers and foundations to connect out-of-work and out-of-school youths with employment opportunities. (An adjunct benefit is that employers also receive an improved pipeline of talent.) Its goal is to engage at least 100,000 young people in apprenticeships, internships, and part- and full-time jobs by 2018, at nearly 30 employers like Target, T-Mobile, Hyatt, and J. C. Penney. Companies in the network have a chance to learn best practices for locating and employing what are called "opportunity youth," to create efficiencies in recruitment and retention, and to gain easier access to pipelines of talent operated by allied nonprofit organizations. So far, the initiative is operating in four cities—Seattle, Los Angeles, Chicago, and Phoenix—and has attracted support from such private philanthropies as the Joyce Foundation, the W. K. Kellogg Foundation, the Schultz Family Foundation, and the Rockefeller Foundation.

Similarly, LeadersUp is an employer-led coalition that keeps a tight focus on giving participating companies a decent return on their investment. Launched in 2013 by the Starbucks Corporation, LeadersUp follows a step-by-step process. It begins with identifying employer needs, then connects employers to candidates in the population of opportunity youth. Finally, the initiative tracks results.

During its first two years in operation, LeadersUp connected over 1,000 youths with employment pathways, engaged more than 30 companies from three economic sectors, and achieved a 60 percent retention rate among new hires. The organization's goal is to connect 5,000 opportunity youth with jobs, at over 100 businesses in ten U.S. markets, by 2017.

Generation USA

Another large effort in early development is the McKinsey Social Initiative's Generation program. Funded by the international management consulting firm McKinsey & Company, Generation's goal is to train and locate job placements for 1 million young people in five countries by 2020. The American portion of the effort is focused on achieving 200,000 placements over five years, focusing on three sectors: technology, health care, and customer service.

In 2015, Generation went live in ten cities across India, Kenya, Mexico, Spain, and the U.S. It has so far graduated 1,200 youths and achieved a 90 percent job placement rate. As of the writing of this guidebook, the U.S. chapter was operating in Florida (Jacksonville and Miami), California (San Jose and San Francisco), Delaware (Wilmington), Georgia (Atlanta), and Pennsylvania (Pittsburgh), with plans to expand its footprint to about 15 more U.S. cities in the near future. Generation USA relies heavily on steering young people into completing industry-recognized credentials. The technology track, for example, leads to CompTIA A+ and CompTIA Network+ certifications, which are well known in the business. These certifications allow typical graduates to work in computer user support or network-support roles at average wages of $18 to $30 per hour. Through the health-care track, young people obtain credentials as certified nurse assistants. The customer service path combines instruction on technical topics with training in interpersonal skills, so graduates will be qualified for jobs in this high-demand field.

Generation USA relies on partnerships with nonprofits such as Goodwill, which provides services that help students stay with the program, and with schools and community colleges in its operating cities. To keep employers interested, involved, and offering positions, the initiative collects detailed statistics on the bottom-line effects of well-trained young people, which can include things like improved profits and decreased turnover. Employer partners so far include hospitals, grocery-store chains, hotels, and retail outlets.

Generation USA is also working to attract young people and give them reasons to enroll in the program. One example is using data from the Gallup Wellness Index to show millennials that improving one's job skill levels brings multiple life benefits. This is an area where donors might be able to help. Philanthropic backing for the Generation program also includes entities like the Walmart Foundation and the Sobrato Family Foundation.

> 600,000 skilled production jobs were unfilled because employers couldn't find qualified candidates.

New Skills at Work

Another mammoth corporate initiative is funded primarily by financial giant JPMorgan Chase. Called New Skills at Work, it is a five-year, $250 million plan. There are three central goals: support better data collection in this area, aid employer demand for middle-skill jobs, and create supply by training new technical workers.

Launched in December 2013, the initiative contributed $50 million in its first year to nonprofits in more than 130 cities worldwide. Within the U.S., New Skills at Work operates in 38 states, including 12 major metro regions where it has made investments topping $1 million or more. JPMC makes decisions on where to invest based on the size of their own corporate footprint—so Los Angeles, San Francisco, Denver, Seattle, Houston, Dallas, Chicago, and Miami dominate the market.

New Skills at Work collaborates with other groups interested in workforce development, including the National Academy Foundation,

Aspen Institute, Jobs for the Future, National Fund for Workforce Solutions, Year Up, and YouthBuild USA. The initiative seeks to close achievement gaps and wage divides by analyzing what skills are missing in local job markets, targeting investments to local nonprofits and schools that have shown they can be effective vocational educators, and encouraging cross-sector cooperation and information sharing.

One snapshot of the program's effectiveness is in Houston. Along with the Greater Houston Partnership and Shell Oil Company, JPMC created UpSkill Houston, a five-year plan to involve businesses, schools, and nonprofits in expanding the amount of good middle-skill work done in the Space City. JPMC donated $250,000 for that planning, part of its total $5 million pledge to the city. The project aims to make core economic sectors in the city—including petrochemical, construction, and health-care work—more efficient and productive.

One product, for instance, is a career-action platform that traces the availability of jobs in the local petrochemical sector. "You can see how an entry-level job is connected to a high-skill, higher-paying job, and understand that if you take the entry-level job, then earn additional credentials and certifications, you can move up the ladder," notes Chauncy Lennon, head of workforce initiatives for JPMorgan Chase.

Grads of Life

One campaign on the cutting edge of making sure employers are on board and participating actively is Grads of Life. Its mission is to make the practical business case for expanding access to middle-skill jobs, for instance by hiring opportunity youth. A major goal is changing the perceptions of some employers that a college degree is the best marker as to which young people should be hired. Grads of Life principal Elyse Rosenblum says "our major goal is to catalyze employer demand" for hires with focused career and technical credentials.

The campaign identifies employers in the local community who need a consistent pipeline of new talent. It then helps employers find local nonprofits, schools, faith-based organizations, and government entities that can provide such employees. The group has used $43 million of donated advertising media, courtesy of the Ad Council and Arnold Worldwide, to support its efforts. The W. K. Kellogg Foundation has been an important funder, as have the Annie Casey, Gap, Rockefeller, and JPMorgan Chase foundations.

Lessons from training run by specific corporations

From a meta perspective, large-scale corporate initiatives are instructive for demonstrating best approaches to partnerships, collaborations, and evaluation. But in-house corporate CTE training programs go a step beyond by showing, in vivid color, how opportunities are unleashed for young people in tangible ways. In the following pages are case studies of five for-profit companies that have fine-tuned excellent training programs within their own four walls.

Toyota

At Toyota Motor Corporation's sprawling plant in Georgetown, Kentucky, a lot more is happening than turning out hundreds of thousands of new cars each year. Toyota is also minting highly skilled, eminently employable young people destined for high-paying, successful careers in advanced manufacturing.

Toyota's Advanced Manufacturing Technician (AMT) program is one of the finest examples of an employer-sponsored effort to raise the skill level of new workers to the high standards needed by today's best manufacturers. Housed at the largest Toyota manufacturing facility outside Japan, the program recruits high-school students to spend three days every week in the company's advanced manufacturing center—a 12,000 square foot building meant to emulate a real manufacturing floor. The process is intensive, instructive, and fun. And life-changing for many participants.

Toyota created this training after realizing that too few skilled technicians existed in the pool of people applying for Toyota jobs to sustain high-quality production. Lots of other companies have come to the same conclusion. In 2011, Deloitte and the Advanced Manufacturing Institute estimated that 600,000 skilled-production and production-support jobs were unfilled because employers couldn't find qualified candidates. "We aren't coming to a crisis within the manufacturing industry," says the director of Toyota's program, Dennis Parker. "We've already entered a workforce crisis."

Starting in the elementary and middle-school years, AMT helps expose students to STEM, technology, and manufacturing work through Project Lead The Way. High-school students who enroll in the AMT program then get a full-immersion experience. They end up with, in addition to their high-school degree, an associate degree in advanced manufacturing automation technology from a local college. They gain invaluable real-world experience at a top company. And they get paid. The program also instructs them in professional behavior.

"We've changed the learning environment," Parker says. "We don't think classrooms are very effective environments. They're not realistic to the real world, so when we partner with a college, they agree to set up an open emulation of the manufacturing environment." The program runs on a normal business schedule of eight-hour days—two where the kids are in class, and three where they are on the floor in an internship. Again mirroring a normal business environment, there is no summer break.

After completing the two-year program, students have three options for further training: a skilled technical internship leading directly to job, an engineering degree, or a bachelor's degree focused on the manufacturing business. To maximize flexibility and independence, AMT doesn't accept government support. And it's selective about which colleges it partners with. The program uses a standardized curriculum across all eight states in which it has a presence. The program begins by knowing how many job slots they have to fill, and recruit carefully so they end up with excellent workers.

> We don't think classrooms are very effective
> learning environments. They're not realistic.

A big bonus: Students make enough money as they go to pay for future college costs (or something else if they choose). Those enrolled in the program earn between $12 and $19 per hour. Graduates hired right out of school will be paid $60,000-$70,000. Three quarters of AMT graduates finish their postsecondary training completely debt free, Parker notes.

What Toyota created in Georgetown has since blossomed to seven other states—West Virginia, Indiana, Minnesota, Texas, Tennessee, Alabama, and Missouri—and 180 companies. Toyota shared its knowledge with the Federation for Advanced Manufacturing Education, and in 2010 a joint AMT/FAME program began. This replicates across a variety of industries Toyota's success at minting productive new workers with valuable skills. As of 2016, there are 19 AMT/FAME programs in operation. Eight of those are directly affiliated with the company that birthed the program; the remainder extend Toyota's method to new firms and places.

There are several way donors could support the Toyota AMT/FAME program. One is by funding Project Lead The Way and other high-quality

STEM education efforts. Philanthropists can also invest in the community colleges that partner with AMT/FAME.

Southwire

Southwire, a privately owned company with close to $6 billion of annual sales and a 7,500-employee workforce, is America's leading manufacturer of wire and cable used for electricity distribution and transmission. Its owners wanted to make substantial gifts to career and technical education, but didn't want to do so through traditional foundation giving. So they decided to use their business itself to create a model that can easily be replicated across the country in small businesses.

Southwire's 12 for Life program locates high-school students at risk of dropping out. Then it helps them complete their education, using the promise and potential of tech jobs. Participants are exposed to a real-world manufacturing environment, and the responsibilities and opportunities of an actual job.

Based in Georgia, Southwire launched the 12 for Life program in partnership with the Carroll County schools (located southwest of Atlanta) and the Florence City Schools (in northern Alabama). Starting in 2004, students were allowed to attend high school part-time and work shifts in an operating manufacturing plant. Southwire purchased a dedicated building for the Georgia-based program in 2006, and the next year a first cohort of 71 students began to participate in a more structured program. By 2009, the effort had met with so much success that Southwire purchased another building in Florence and mirrored the curriculum there. Southwire invested about $4 million to launch the program.

Students attend class part of every school day and then work a four-hour shift in the plant. According to Southwire, students learn "a variety of job skills, including machine operation, logistics, product and reel assembly, shipping, quality assurance and data entry." They must be at least 16 years old, pass a drug-screening test, and have been identified by their district as needing assistance to graduate from high school. To help them earn their high-school degree, students receive credit for time on the job.

This isn't merely an after-school pocket-money job. Students are immersed in the culture of Southwire and are considered part-time employees responsible for participating in company life. They are paired with mentors inside the company who guide them in many ways. In addition to teaching concrete job skills, the program helps young men and women learn how to manage their money, file and pay taxes, satisfy bosses, and work hard as a member of a team. It also convinces partici-pants—students at high risk of dropping out—to remain in school and keep studying.

Results are promising. By mid-2015, more than 1,100 students have graduated from the program. Of these, 40 percent were able to go on to postsecondary education, 20 percent became full-time employees at Southwire, and 30 percent were accepted into the U.S. military.

Penn Medicine
The largest employer in the Philadelphia area, Penn Medicine, with 18,000 employees, created a vocational-technical initiative in 2007. What began as a summer program has evolved into an intensive, multiyear initiative in partnership with three high schools located in economically disadvantaged areas of Philadelphia. The program introduces young peo-ple in striking detail to career opportunities in the medical field.

Beginning in their junior year of high school, students take college-level courses, get job placements throughout the Penn Medicine system, and receive professional development instruction and coaching through mentorships. The program continues through the senior year. During the two-year high-school portion of the program students earn minimum wage and are on the job 10-15 hours per week. After they graduate from high school, students enter an internship, within which they are simultaneously enrolled in college and working 20 hours per week at a Penn Medicine facility. They are paid for a full 40-hour workweek, and their hourly wage jumps to about $18 an hour.

Entering students "really don't know the diversity of jobs and careers and opportunities available in health care," reports Frances Graham, Penn Medicine's director of workforce development. Through careful selection, the Penn Medicine program has been able to maintain a 100 percent graduation rate, despite the tough backgrounds of many stu-dents in the participating high schools. Graduates of the program take up jobs in the medical field paying $16 to $18 per hour.

Dow Chemical
Dow Chemical, one of the 50 largest U.S. corporations, created an in-house apprenticeship program in 2015. The company hired about 50 young apprentices for placement across five locations—three facilities in Texas, one in California, and one in Michigan. Like other examples, Dow's program combines classroom training with on-the-job instruction.

Their effort last for three years. During that period, apprentices are paid on a full-time, 40-hour-per-week schedule for the combination of work, classroom time, and personal study that they put in.

At the completion of the apprenticeship program, graduates will have an associate degree from a local community college and a valuable track record of work experience. Those wanting to stay at Dow will be funneled immediately into one of two technical career paths at the company. Dow Chemical recruits candidates for this program from high schools, and also markets it to individuals transitioning out of the military.

The Gap

As one of the largest clothing retailers in the U.S., Gap Inc. has significant experience hiring young, first-time workers. Beginning in 2007, the company's foundation decided to parlay that expertise into an initiative that helps young people increase their skills above the entry level. Called This Way Ahead, the program provides training and internships for disadvantaged youth in ten U.S. cities (plus two in the United Kingdom).

This Way Ahead partners with nonprofits in targeted cities (including Goodwill, the Door, Enterprise for High School Students, and others, all of which depend on donor support) to present eight different workshops in various aspects of career training. At the conclusion of the training, youths interview for paid internships in stores across the corporate clothing empire (including Old Navy, Banana Republic, and Gap stores). The paid internship is ten weeks in duration, with 12 hours of work per week. Three fourths of the young people who start the training secure an internship.

"We found this combination of training from a nonprofit, coupled with a real working, paid experience structured as an internship, was successful," says Gail Gershon of the Gap Foundation. "The results were so positive that our brands agreed to help us expand. We've found that our hired employees who started with This Way Ahead have double the retention rate of their peers, they have higher engagement scores, and they've turned into a great resource of talent."

Funding Job-prep
Nonprofits

Corresponding with piqued interest in career and
technical education from corporations, a growing
roster of nonprofit organizations have developed
training programs over the past few decades. These
present prime investment opportunities for donors.

Nonprofits are particularly effective at reaching
middle- and low-performing youth and convincing
them of the benefits of learning while working,
thereby pulling into successful lives many individuals

who otherwise would have languished or drifted into trouble. "Kids from low-income families particularly need these opportunities to earn as they go to school," says Allison Gerber of the Annie E. Casey Foundation, because many lack the family and community supports that help middle-class youths edge their way into careers.

Supporting a strong existing nonprofit program—or launching a new one in your location—could become a key part of your investment portfolio. This chapter offers a handful of instructive models.

Genesys Works and Year Up
Two often-cited workforce development nonprofits for youth are Genesys Works and Year Up.

Genesys Works builds both technical and soft skills that prepare the "quiet middle" of American youth for middle-class jobs. The program has a technical focus that includes training in accounting, drafting, engineering, IT, and cybersecurity. The organization currently operates in Houston, the Twin Cities, Chicago, and the Bay Area, with another site scheduled to open in Washington, D.C., in 2016.

Young people enter the program the summer prior to their senior year in high school. After eight weeks of intensive training, they are given a yearlong part-time job with one of many business partners. These are paid positions with significant duties and chances to earn valuable experience.

One of the organization's chief goals is to ensure that students go on to postsecondary achievement, and 95 percent of their graduates ultimately do. Fully 86 percent of Genesys grads persist in postsecondary training beyond the second year. When they hit the work force, their average starting employment wage is around $41,000.

Year Up was launched in Boston in 2000, with the task of helping 18- to 24-year-olds who had earned a high-school diploma or GED but lacked further direction in life or career. High-school guidance counselors, organizations like Big Brothers Big Sisters, and the YMCA help identify candidates. It can be a tricky clientele: many are Spanish-speaking, have an average high-school GPA of just 1.9, and the typical SAT score is 780. One crucial screen: Participants must be "at-risk but not high-risk"—that is, participants cannot use drugs or have committed violent crimes.

The program can be tough. It requires a detailed application, a writing sample, references, and two interviews. For every 100 young adults who say they are interested, only 25 will complete the application process, and only ten will be accepted. Participants must sign an agreement that stipulates immediate expulsion for drug use, and a lower stipend for being even one minute late to class. Those accepted receive six months of full-time training. If they make it through that, they begin a six-month internship at a corporate partner.

Year Up emphasizes professional and technical skills. For instance, IT training and work can cover duties like desktop and network computer support, hardware repair, software installation, virus and malware protection, and application support. Participants get staff advising on personal as well as professional issues, and they are assigned a mentor from the business community.

Students receive a $30-a-day stipend for living expenses while they are training (though they lose $25 of that if they are late for class). Once they begin working they get a weekly stipend of roughly $200, paid by the corporate partners, who also help Year Up itself defray roughly $2,000 out of the $11,000 annual cost per student. (The remaining expenses are covered by foundations, companies, and individual supporters.)

> Just 18 percent of graduating computer-science majors are female. This nonprofit is trying to change that.

The goal is that once the Year Up training is complete, each participant will be hired by the company where he or she interned. Even when this doesn't happen, the participant has a new toolbox of skills and a working track record that can be taken to the next career opportunity. He or she also earns between 18 and 30 college credit hours for completing the program.

Four months after graduating, 84 percent of Year Up participants are either working or attending college full time. The average wage of workers is $16 per hour. That's 30 percent more than was earned by a control group of peers outside the program.

Kim Tanner of the Jenesis Group (a Dallas-based linchpin funder of Genesys Works) notes that organizations like Year Up and Genesys Works are changing corporate perceptions of youth who don't have a four-year college degree. "These are kids capable of doing great work. They just need opportunities and training," she says.

JobsFirstNYC

JobsFirstNYC was founded in 2006 by the Tiger Foundation and the New York City Workforce Funders Group to connect disengaged, unemployed, out-of-school youth ages 18 to 24 to the business world. Their mechanism is a sectoral emphasis that prepares students and then places them in very specific technical jobs that are undersupplied. JobsFirstNYC does not provide direct training and placements. Rather, it organizes, funds, and incubates partner organizations that do this work, including the Lower East Side Employment Network, Bronx Opportunity Network, Restaurant Industry Partnership, and Young Adult Sectoral Employment Project.

Take, for instance, the Young Adult Sectoral Employment Project, which launched in 2013. It collaborates with businesses in industries and occupations that are short on particular kinds of trained workers. These include construction and maintenance jobs, theater technicians, employees for New York's hospitality industry, and IT workers. The project offers young people the right kind of tightly focused instruction, and then funnels them into partner employers.

JobsFirstNYC has recently been supported by the Achelis and Bodman Foundations, the Annie E. Casey Foundation, the Heckscher Foundation for Children, the Pinkerton Foundation, and many others. Laurie Dien of the Pinkerton Foundation cites close collaboration with real-world employers as the key to success in the JobsFirst young adult sectoral strategy. "It's high engagement with an employer—determining what their needs are—and then matching that to training to those needs by a community partner," she summarizes.

In addition to working hand-in-glove with employers, and then building good training that prepares clients for technical jobs, JobsFirstNYC also serves as a type of "think tank" on youth unemployment. It publishes reports and papers. It hosts speakers, and otherwise increases public awareness and understanding of what is necessary to succeed in drawing marginal workers into prosperous employment.

Girls Who Code

In 1984, 38 percent of all computer-science majors were women. Today, just 18 percent of graduating computer-science majors are female. In 2012, Reshma Saujani created a nonprofit aimed at reducing that imbalance, while at the same time reducing the deepening shortage of qualified programmers in the U.S. The U.S. Department of Labor estimates that by 2020, there will be 1.4 million unfilled computer-specialist jobs at American businesses.

Saujani's group, Girls Who Code, hopes that wider exposure to computer programming in high school can ignite an interest within young women to pursue the field as a vocation. Girls Who Code thus conducts summer immersion programs and workshops throughout the U.S. The charity's goal is to instruct 1 million girls in computer programming by the year 2020.

The summer immersion program is designed for sophomores and juniors in high school. Free of charge, the intensive seven-week venture helps participants explore different aspects of computer science. These include website development, mobile-app development, and robotics programming. Among graduates of the summer Girls Who Code immersion program, 90 percent go on to pursue postsecondary education with a focus on computer science.

Entry standards are fairly rigorous: Participants must commit to attending the program every weekday, 9 a.m. to 4 p.m., for seven weeks, simulating a business schedule. Only two absences are permitted during that period. Girls Who Code also sponsors local clubs aimed at girls in sixth to twelfth grade, and the nonprofit trains community volunteers to teach young women in these settings. Most clubs have 10-30 members. They are asked to meet for 8 hours per month, which allows each club to work through 40 hours of curriculum each year.

Girls Who Code enjoys the support of many corporate sponsors, including the Adobe Foundation, Microsoft, GE, the Verizon Wireless Foundation, Twitter, and Capital One. The Annie E. Casey Foundation has also been an important supporter. In 2014 the organization received a $1 million grant from AT&T. In addition, 20 large companies have offered paid internships and other opportunities to graduates of Girls Who Code. These include major corporations like Goldman Sachs and Microsoft.

Woodlawn Cemetery Preservation Training Program
Historic Woodlawn Cemetery, located in the upper Bronx, covers more than 400 acres. It includes 1,300 mausoleums and 150,000 monuments. Among these are the graves of such notables as Herman Melville, Joseph Pulitzer, and J. C. Penney.

Since the summer of 2015, an unusual sight has caught the attention of some of Woodlawn's many visitors—youths in bright orange shirts, dutifully restoring and preserving dozens of monuments and headstones.

Twelve young adults were enrolled in a new Woodlawn Cemetery Preservation Training Program. This nine-week internship has the dual purpose of helping to preserve and restore the cemetery while offering disadvantaged youths hands-on training in the craft of stonemasonry.

"Historic cemeteries are in a losing battle of maintaining today's overwhelming number of monuments, amid limited interest in care from descendants," says Woodlawn's historian, Susan Olsen. "Using our historic cemetery as a training site, or 'outdoor lab,' is a way to address the issue."

Woodlawn hired a trainer and recruited at-risk youths aged 18 to 24 from local high schools and social-service agencies. Of 30 initial applicants, 12 were admitted to the pilot program. For two months, these interns received a combination of classroom instruction and hands-on activity in the cemetery. They were paid $10 per hour, for a 30-hour workweek, throughout their internship,

The workers-in-training labored alongside resident stone craftsman Robert Cappiello and learned the skills of the trade. They started with measuring and photographing stones, cleaning monuments, sculptures, and mausoleums, and resetting gravestones. "I taught the basic safety skills, terminologies, stone types, and hand skills needed to be in this trade," notes Cappiello. The ninth week of the program culminated in a visit to the training center of the International Masonry Institute in Long Island City, where the interns completed OSHA training and took certification tests.

With a keystone grant from the Heckscher Foundation for Children, interns also benefited from weekly life-skills classes run by Opportunities for a Better Tomorrow, a Bronx-based nonprofit profiled later in this chapter. "We wanted to be as creative as we could in addressing all the life issues these young people are facing," says Frank Sanchis of the World Monuments Fund—a preservation nonprofit that hopes to make the Woodlawn pilot a model for other programs across the country.

Although the program is young, its results are promising. In the first cohort, 11 of the 12 students completed the nine weeks of training; eight of those interns are now employed directly in the masonry trade, including three who continued at Woodlawn Cemetery in a deeper 19-month paid apprenticeship program. "These young people are now working in jobs at good salaries—most are making $45,000 a year with benefits," says Sanchis.

The biggest obstacle to replication of this program may be the high cost per youth served. John Krieger of the Achelis and Bodman Foundations, which offered the Woodlawn program a $30,000 grant, was willing to provide seed capital because of the coalition of partners. "The fact that so many high-quality organizations were willing to participate gave us confidence." A second cohort of preservation interns is expected at Woodlawn in the summer of 2016, and Sanchis is now searching for suitable cemeteries in other parts of the U.S. where a similar program could be launched.

Opportunities for a Better Tomorrow
In the early 1980s, a community board in the Sunset Park area of Brooklyn asked Sister Mary Franciscus, a Catholic-school principal, to form an organization to address the high number of student dropouts in the neighborhood. Sister Franciscus founded Opportunities for a Better Tomorrow in 1983, and today the organization continues to follow her model for job training and life transformation: twenty weeks of intensive instruction in business skills, high-school equivalency degree instruction, job placement services, and ongoing post-employment follow up.

OBT zeroes in on high-risk kids without a high-school diploma. Like Genesys Works and Year Up, it is demanding, with a training atmosphere meant to reflect the realities of a corporate office. Students must clock in each day, dress professionally, and complete assignments on schedule. The training includes business math, business English, office procedures, computer classes, public speaking and communications, and a world-of-work module.

"A lot of our emphasis is experiential," notes CEO Randy Peers. "School didn't work for these young adults, so we don't structure things as if it were school. Everything is made to seem like a corporate office. We have a dress code, code of conduct, make assignments, and have performance evaluations."

The nonprofit offers several specific credentialing and career-training pathways. A fairly new one is designed to feed New York City's growing IT infrastructure—an intensive 10-week-long website design and coding session. Before they enroll students must graduate from high school or earn a GED. Instruction in HTML, JavaScript, and Adobe Photoshop is part of the curriculum. All students build their own websites, and contribute to design websites for local community organizations and businesses.

A second technical pathway preps students to become medical administrative assistants via certification from the National Health Career Association. Trainees must again first graduate from high school. Then they are taught medical basics, medical terminology, and instructed in communications, customer service, and basic bookkeeping. Trainees get an internship in a medical business.

Through other tracks, students can also obtain a Microsoft Office certification and a National Retail Federation customer service certification. New entrants take an aptitude test to see which credentialing path they would most logically fit into. The program also offers opportunities from direct entry into employment.

OBT has successfully ushered many disconnected young people into meaningful work. It has a strong reputation among financial-services employers in New York City. Many graduates begin working in retail banks or corporate mailroom operations at firms such as Morgan Stanley, Moody's, Greenberg Traurig, or Random House. Other graduates pursue postsecondary training, often as the first members of their family to do so.

> School didn't work for these young adults, so we don't structure things as if it were school. Everything is made to seem like a corporate office.

In 2010, OBT identified southeastern Queens as a prime location for expansion, due to a high population of troubled youth. OBT was on the cusp of launching a fundraising campaign for the expansion when the area YMCA approached them with a proposal. It had a similar vision for reaching people in the region, and already had the buildings and infrastructure in the area that OBT would require. So the two nonprofits ended up partnering together to create the Y Roads Center.

OBT conducts its training within a building where the YMCA provides other wraparound services—everything from mental-health counseling to basic YMCA recreation classes. The startup thus cost $800,000, versus an estimated $2 million if OBT had launched the new center on its own. The partnership has been so successful that OBT and the YMCA opened a second site in 2012 in the Jamaica-area of Queens and a third in the Bronx in 2014. "It's been a cost-effective way for us to expand, since the Y handles the infrastructure cost," says Peers.

In another collaboration, OBT began expanding its computer-programming track in 2015 by linking arms with Industry City, a private real-estate development that is renovating old industrial buildings in the original neighborhood where OBT started, then leasing them to tech firms and other tenants. OBT is in the process of building an innovation lab in the complex where it can offer technical training to students who then will have opportunities to slide into jobs at the for-profit tech firms moving into Industry City. Students who want to continue beyond the level of tech training OBT offers will be handed off by the nonprofit to the New York City College of Technology.

"Our aim is that these kids get classroom training and do an internship with one of the firms on site," according to Peers. "We want to expose them to opportunities they haven't considered before. We do that in big ways and in little ways—but over the 20 weeks, it has an impact."

The Robin Hood Foundation has been the biggest individual charitable funder of Opportunities for a Better Tomorrow. Crucial support has also come from the Tiger Foundation and the Achelis and Bodman Foundations. Mark Foggin is a management consultant and individual OBT donor who grew up in a blue-collar household and understands the importance and potential of work-based pathways to learning. He describes the organization's model for leading young New Yorkers to improve their talents and move themselves out of poverty as inspiring.

Hope Builders

Jumping across the U.S. to California, Hope Builders (formerly known as Taller San Jose) exemplifies a nonprofit that has long focused on getting difficult populations into entry-level work, but also grasped the importance of upskilling as a way of keeping workers progressing up the economic ladder. CEO Shawna Smith says the Great Recession taught her organization the importance of middle-credential jobs. Now her team emphasizes job placement for entry-level work, but also credentialing and postsecondary learning that is important to job advancement.

Hope Builders is working in a challenging arena—the troubled youth of Orange County, California. It operates a 28-month program that offers the young people most at risk in its community a proven route to job success. There is a mix of coaching, skill building, job placement, assistance with job retention, and continuing education. In its training academies Hope Builders focuses on instruction in construction, health care, and business skills. Participants also receive personal counseling and instruction.

When its participants are ready to reach for middle-skill jobs, Hope Builders partners with local institutions like Santa Ana College, medical trainers, and Tierra Institute International. These offer college credits or occupational credentials in practical areas like office management, blood-drawing, and solar-panel installation.

Fully 57 percent of Hope Builders graduates go on to attain a postsecondary certificate, degree, or apprenticeship. The group keeps in touch with participants for two years after they complete the program in order to improve rates of job retention and advancement. It is an explicit goal of the effort that students eventually continue their education through a postsecondary certificate, a six-month apprenticeship, or at least 12 units of college coursework.

"We're now looking at some additional industries where we might develop other training," says Smith. "One is in advanced skills manufacturing. Another is dental assisting."

Project L.I.F.T.
For a licensed clinical psychologist, Bob Zaccheo keeps an unusual home office, filled with bicycles, appliances, boats, a textile-printing machine, and even a classic Ford Model T automobile. These artifacts all connect to physical labor, require tinkering and repair, and appeal to the hunger of many young men to work with their hands on tangible products. Having them as unorthodox tools has helped Zaccheo meet with much greater success as a social worker than he ever could have from a counselor's chair.

From Stuart, Florida, Zaccheo runs a nonprofit called Project L.I.F.T. It was born out of his frustration with the obstacles to success in a traditional social-work clinic. As a therapist, Zaccheo discovered firsthand that young men in particular were reluctant to open up about struggles with alcoholism, drug abuse, depression, and anxiety. So he traded in his desk and dress shirts and ties for a pair of work boots, rented a nearby garage, and spent time working with his patients repairing vehicles. This hands-on experience built trust while yielding learning, and mixed with more conventional individual and group therapy it proved able to produce real life change.

"What I quickly realized was that I could get information really fast under the hood of a car that I couldn't get sitting in a clinical office," Zaccheo says.

Project L.I.F.T. officially launched in 2010 with the mission of using vocational trades—car, boat, bicycle, and appliance restoration and repair—to give young men practical job skills, and ween them off addictive substances. In the early days, Zaccheo helped 19 kids through the program while continuing his day job as a therapist for the state of Florida. Eventually he began devoting his full attention to the nonprofit.

Project L.I.F.T. has since blossomed. It recently opened a new 8,000-square-foot facility offering 11 different vocational tracts. It employs three full-time therapists, seven vocational instructors, and 13 volunteers. Trades in which students are instructed include boat building, auto repair, carpentry, pipefitting, welding, printing, and bike repair.

Indian River State College approached Zaccheo about using Project L.I.F.T. as a feeder program to its occupational-certification courses. "That partnership has been really nice," he reports. "It's developed to the point where the college wants to bring its instructors down to our shop and provide on-site training for certifications."

> The project uses vocational trades—car, boat, bicycle, and appliance repair—to give young men practical job skills and ween them off addictive substances.

One thing that makes Project L.I.F.T. unusual is the virtuous cycle of charity it creates. Individuals from the community donate their goods to the nonprofit. Zaccheo and his team of recovering youths repair and restore them. Then the goods are either sold (with the profits funneled back into the organization) or donated to needy individuals. Some restored bikes, for instance, are donated to local homeless men and women. Project L.I.F.T. recently gave a repaired car for a single mom.

The program targets teenage males between the ages of 13 and 19, most with a criminal past, often drug-related. "These are the kids that are using two to three drugs at a time—alcohol, marijuana, cocaine, synthetic opiates, even heroin," reports Zaccheo. In addition to vocational training they get comprehensive mental-health therapy, including substance abuse counseling and group and individual treatment. To create tighter-knit relationships, the team participates in a family-style meal every night. For the young men it enrolls, the transition from addict to worker to giver can be monumental. "It changes the whole cast of their mind," says Zaccheo.

The program maintains a sobriety success rate of 79-84 percent. The graduation rate is the same, because being sober is a condition of graduating. Three quarters of participants stay out of the criminal-justice system after graduating.

Project L.I.F.T. plans to start serving young women in the future. Zaccheo is also evaluating expansion beyond at-risk youth, to a more general population. "If we can teach these guys to become successful, taxpaying citizens in our community, then maybe we could teach anybody to do that," he suggests.

The Hobe Sound Community Chest is one satisfied supporter of the nonprofit. A conglomeration of 500 private donors who raise $1.5 million annually to support 40 humanitarian agencies in the area, the Community Chest makes an annual $25,000 grant to Project L.I.F.T. "When Bob talks with you about the organization's mission, he sounds almost like a venture entrepreneur," explains HSCC board member Joe Frelinghuysen. "But it's not about making money, it's about saving lives. He's passionate about the mission."

HSCC donors also volunteered to help Zaccheo and his team relocate to their new shop. Frelinghuysen and others have donated used cars. It pleased Frelinghuysen to watch kids fix up his donation and sell it for $5,000, then apply those funds to the new building expansion. "My goal through charitable giving has been to do something with real impact," he notes. "Not just writing a check, but making an impact. Here, I can."

Working Through Community Colleges

For donors who want to improve and expand career and technical education, working through community colleges should hold wide appeal. Community colleges allow donors to go beyond just serving young people, for instance, because they are also used by many adults to increase their skill levels mid-career. In many locales, the community college is also one of the better managed and more practical public institutions. Since their very genesis, community colleges have aimed to connect their students directly to work. So the best community colleges tend to offer a kind of gold standard when it comes to vocational education.

Yet community colleges have an image problem. More than 12,000 such schools exist across the U.S., and these institutions educate over half of students in the country, but many are known for high dropout rates, lackluster academics, or irrelevant degrees. Some Americans, projecting what Monty Sullivan, president of the Louisiana Technical and College System, calls a "caste view," perceive community colleges as warehousing poor-performing students who aren't smart enough to enter four-year schools.

Many of these stigmas grow out of misperceptions or out-of-date understandings. Still others persist due to the huge number of mediocre community colleges across the nation. However, among those, there are stellar numbers of community colleges that produce job-ready graduates in an extraordinarily time-efficient, cost-effective process. Among other contributions, outstanding community colleges elevate many Americans from low-income backgrounds who would otherwise be stuck in ruts of low-wage, menial work. And many local business leaders will tell you that the track record of their nearby community college is more important to the economic health of their region than the most prestigious colleges.

Strong community colleges can be great equalizers in America. James Denova of the Benedum Foundation calls these local laboratories of learning "one of the best anti-poverty programs in the U.S.," and points to their "affordability, open enrollment, remediation, and social supports for people who aren't prepared for postsecondary education by our high-school system." He adds, "I think we're entering the era of community colleges. They've certainly started to get more recognition and respect in the last ten years."

Donor Carrie Morgridge suggests that four-year schools can learn much from the adaptability, cost-control, and success with hard populations of well-run community colleges. "Higher education is going to have to have this huge makeover to catch up with what community colleges are now doing," she says. "Community colleges are a powerful tool. We've found they are hungry to work in the communities in which they serve."

Community colleges are an invention of America's democratic tradition. "The community college is the only U.S.-born higher education institution," notes Eduardo Padron, president of Miami Dade College in south Florida. They remain today an almost exclusively American phenomenon.

Community colleges also offer one of today's commonest portals into well-paying technology jobs. Continuing to excel at this task will allow community colleges to upend many traditional biases against two-year schools.

An important test of an effective community college is ensuring that learners actually leave with a degree or useful certification. Current statistics leave much room for improvement. Completion rates in many associate-degree programs hover around 30 percent. Many schools have miles to go to improve these ratios.

> We have the most powerful economy in the world for putting unskilled people into jobs. The problem is that these jobs can be hard to move up from.

Also, too many community colleges are willing to coast along enrolling students in old-fashioned, low-paying fields that lack much career potential. Sometimes this is driven by administrators who would rather shape their institutions in a conventional academic mold and transfer their students on to other colleges, instead of operating as twenty-first century employment engines. "Many community colleges remain primarily focused on their traditional mission of simply feeding students into the four-year colleges, rather than training individuals for the workforce," says economist Harry Holzer of the Brookings Institution.

Donors should understand that career and technical training and career pathways don't preclude students from going on to obtain higher degrees. To the contrary, getting serious about a vocation is often the starting point for further study. The key is to give students choices. One can earn a credential and happily jump off the train there, or go on to complete an associate degree, or become a full-fledged engineer, chemist, or doctor. Career education focuses students on succeeding in school, whatever the terminus.

"The language and message needs to be about career pathways," urges Denova. "It's not about community college versus four-year programs.

It's helping students choose a career path that has different levels they might pursue at different points in their lives."

If donors can help community colleges become practical connectors of people to work, many good overflow effects will result, argues Sandy Shugart, president of Orlando's Valencia College:

> If you want to change a family, you have to change the circumstances of the head of the household. Very often I hear if you want to fix everything, you need to start at birth, or preschool. But the way to change a two-year-old's experience is to change the mom's experience. We need to focus on young adults who have a family to raise. If we change their economic trajectory with short, low-opportunity-cost training—particularly in an era when we have deep, pervasive skill shortages in areas that lend themselves to training—that's the way to really make a difference in American life.

Donor-supported community college efforts that lead the way

There are more than 1,000 community colleges in the U.S. Donors who want a handy list of good ones to study can look up the Aspen Institute's annual prize for community college excellence. It carries a $1 million award, and is given out every other year. The organization's 2015 top pick was Santa Fe College in Gainesville, Florida, and the selection committee also honored nine runners-up.

The most career-oriented colleges integrate their course offerings with employer needs in their community. Rather than just offering an undifferentiated cafeteria menu of options, effective schools emphasize targeted courses of proven value, and provide a clear roadmap and guidance to get students from start to completion.

Miami Dade College in south Florida, for instance, has a current focus on the regional need for data analysts, air traffic controllers, animation and game developers, and physician assistants. When the college first noticed the growing gaming and animation industry in the Miami area, it sent a group to analyze Pixar Studios in California. The research team reported back, and the college created an animation and gaming program that includes a collaboration among Viacom, Nickelodeon, Disney, and Sony Pictures. Graduates earn an associate of science degree in computer-programming analysis, with a specialization in either gaming or animation, and can expect to earn at least $75,000 to $80,000 per year. Miami Dade is supported by an active foundation that collects philanthropic donations and distributes the money to college priorities—$11 million of donations in the latest year.

Colorado Mountain College, which has attracted the support of the Morgridge Family Foundation, provides career training at many of its 11 campuses scattered across the north-central Rocky Mountains. The college has partnered with local industries and public schools to build programs in electrical trades, welding, culinary arts, and more. The college operates an apprenticeship program that trains chefs for the many resort towns in the Rockies. Donor Carrie Morgridge recently funded welding certification courses at the Leadville campus, where that skill is an important part of the mining industry. It is a dual-enrollment program serving high-school seniors, who also earn college credit. The Morgridge Family Foundation commitment over two years was for $75,000.

Lee College in Baytown, Texas, has a partnership with Chevron Phillips Chemical Company for technical training and mentorship that will feed well-credentialed workers into Chevron's nearby Cedar Bayou facility. The Benedum Foundation has established programs with community colleges in West Virginia and southwestern Pennsylvania, like the certificate and degree programs the foundation funded in 2009 at Eastern West Virginia Community & Technical College in wind turbine technology, created to support the burgeoning wind farms in that part of the country. Lorain Community College has established 22 career pathways in over 30 high schools near Cleveland, Ohio, with philanthropic support. Students start taking college classes early in their high-school career, and can complete a bachelor's degree by the age of 20, for 80 percent less than a conventional college track in the area.

Another area of specialization for community colleges is to help adult learners remedy gaps in their education, and then expand their workforce skills. There are many variations of what are known as adult basic education (ABE) programs. Less effective examples require extensive book learning before job-skill training begins, with the result that many learners drop out. There are more effective programs that integrate academic and hands-on instruction right from the beginning, and teach the two areas concurrently.

One top-ranking example is the I-BEST program originally launched at Seattle Central College in 2005. It has now spread statewide, and is being replicated in other states. I-BEST allows adult students to take remedial courses while at the same time working toward a specific workforce credential, certification, or degree—a cocktail that has yielded crisp success.

Launched with financial support from the Lumina and Ford foundations, the program harnesses team teaching by pairing a basic-skills trainer with an academic instructor. These feed students both remedial and technical lessons simultaneously. I-BEST students have proven three times likelier than other adult students to earn college credit, and nine times likelier to earn a work credential.

"I-BEST transformed the way we educate low-income, low-skill, and immigrant adults to ensure their family's empowerment and economic well-being," says Jon Kerr of the Washington State Board for Community & Technical Colleges. "Students are no longer stuck in years of adult basic education and English language classes. They do these things while earning college credits and preparing for work, and learn with more motivation and more understanding."

Two examples of donor investments
in a local community college

During late 2014 and early 2015, the oil and gas industry shed an estimated 100,000 jobs. With that difficult economic backdrop, Karen Wright—CEO of one of the major industrial suppliers to the industry, gas-compressor manufacturer Ariel Corporation—faced a dilemma. She had always striven to never lay off her workforce, partly because she knew that skilled machinists and mechanics are difficult to replace once gone. But with the energy sector is a deep slump, what choice did she have?

A brainstorm made her realize there was an alternative. Rather than lay off employees, she decided to keep her workforce at a full-time 40 hour week, but allow employees to spend a portion of their work time enrolled at a technical college earning an associate degree, either in machine trades or mechanics. Wright and the Ariel Corporation had already laid the groundwork for this decision through intensive, strategic donations to local community colleges and tech schools in preceding years.

"It's partly a strategy to keep our workers busy. But it's also within a long-term vision of growing a valuable workforce, not just for ourselves, but for other manufacturers and for the oil and gas industry overall," Wright told us.

Called a "quiet philanthropist" by the local newspaper, Wright has made a loud impact on the regional economy—through the combination of jobs created at the Ariel Corporation and philanthropic investments in the education infrastructure of central Ohio. She and her team previously developed robust CTE curricula for use in training Ariel employees at Stark State, Central Ohio Technical College, Zane State, and the Knox County Career Center. "It's a partnership where we develop the program for them, they provide the venue, and we pay them for the college credits our workers earn," Wright says.

The Ariel Foundation also makes around $5 million of gifts every year in Wright's hometown of Mount Vernon, Ohio. Recent grants have supported engineering and nursing scholarships at Mount Vernon Nazarene University, and brought STEM training into the local public-school system. Wright aims to give at least 10 percent of her company's annual profits to charitable causes.

> Low-income workers need to see that training leads directly to better work. If they can't see a light at the end of the tunnel, it's too long of a tunnel.

"The more you give, the more you get, so to speak. Your success multiplies," Wright states. "The Bible says 'It's more blessed to give than to receive.' And I find that when you give you receive back tenfold. The joy of giving is real. It actually does result in good things happening from every perspective."

Another female philanthropist with a strong interest in career and technical education is Penny Enroth. Her early investments in the area included a $110,000 grant to Moore County schools in North Carolina to integrate Project Lead The Way into their curriculum. Soon she was working with Sandhills Community College. The college was scheduled to tear down an unused maintenance building on its property when they realized the building could be repurposed as an excellent trades instruction facility. Enroth's Palmer Foundation made an initial investment of $212,000 to fund the renovation and help revive the local economy. Operating in the shadow of the Research Triangle Park 70 miles north, the rural Sandhills region has suffered economically from declines in industry and tobacco farming.

The Palmer Trades Center is now an active venue for students pursuing credentials in production technology, electrical contracting, and advanced welding. The training facility is impressive, and thanks to a grant from the Golden LEAF Foundation it is about to get an entirely new wing that will house machinery for training in computer numerical control machining. Since its trades program launched in 2013, Sandhills has graduated 154 students, with eight out of ten now holding jobs at area manufacturers such as Caterpillar, Unilever, and Butterball. To stay in sync with local businesses Sandhills maintains an advisory committee representing local employers. "We teach what the community needs," notes Andi Korte of Sandhills. "And that has improved hiring rates for our students."

The Palmer Foundation's support for Sandhills now amounts to over half-a-million dollars. This has helped the college attract other grants. The Duke Energy Foundation has now given the college two grants totaling $450,000 combined for CTE education, including one gift that allowed the purchase of a virtual welding machine for training purposes. The Golden LEAF Foundation put up $750,000 for the 4,500 square foot expansion of the Palmer Trades Center. And a corporate donor, Victory Technology, has donated valuable welding equipment and a plasma cutter.

"We're not a large foundation," says Enroth. "But we take risks. And so we're a little fish that attracts bigger fish."

Three other community colleges with CTE bents

Rio Salado College

A premier career-oriented community college located just outside of Phoenix, Rio Salado College serves 57,000 students—30,000 of them online—from a total of 47 states. The largest online community college in the U.S., it offers more than 500 Internet-based courses, and hundreds more in person, in 122 programs of study that lead to 26 associate degrees and 87 different types of certificates. The college also provides strong student services—access to advisers, site-based tutoring, and 13 different regional sites. "Online learning has been criticized in the past for not having enough support services, so we've invested heavily in those to ensure that our students have all the help they need," says president Chris Bustamante.

In particular, RSC strives to channel students either directly into careers, or as transfers into four-year schools. To lead students toward useful end points and careers, the college has created several programs:

- *Rio Compass* is a degree tracker that helps students make sure their class selections lead efficiently to degree completion.

It is supported by funding from the Bill & Melinda Gates Foundation, which also covers predictive analytics, peer mentors, and career coaches.

- *Rio Learn* includes a dashboard that shows students what assignments they need to complete.
- *Rio Pace* allows students to monitor their progress in a course, compare their data to others in the same course, and see if they are on track for success.

Rio gives students many entry and exit points into classes—48 start dates per year mean that scores of new courses begin every week. This helps working adults who enroll to upgrade their skill level. Enrollees flock to its skill centers where they can get short-term three- to four-week training opportunities of that lead to higher-paying jobs.

One group attracted to RSC's combination of flexibility and affordability (courses average $84 per credit hour) is women with children, who make up 60 percent of the student body. Rio Salado also makes special efforts to provide career education to veterans, incarcerated prisoners and ex-offenders, and juvenile delinquents (it served 2,820 incarcerated youth in 2014). Rio provides adult basic education classes to 10,000 high-school dropouts every year. Some of these enroll in a track that allows them to earn up to 25 college credits while finishing their GED.

Rio Salado College has been widely lauded for its accomplishments. A McKinsey & Company report found it to be one of the top eight higher-education institutions in the country in terms of efficiency and productivity. In addition to major funding from the Gates Foundation that helped the college create its online courses and expand its local campuses, Rio has built itself up with support from the Pulliam, Lumina, Carr Family, and Helios Education foundations, the Carstens Family Funds, the Griffith Insurance Education Foundation, and other donors.

Valencia College

Along with the tourist businesses for which it is known, Orlando, Florida, is becoming a home for high-tech industries in aviation, aerospace, and biotechnology. Sandy Shugart, president of Valencia College, describes his city as "a tale of two economies." There are significant numbers of skilled jobs, and lots of entry-level work that is low-paid.

"We have the most powerful economy in the world for putting unskilled people into jobs," Shugart explains. "The problem is that these jobs are hard to move up from. It takes two body lengths to reach the next rung on the ladder."

Valencia College's mission is to add more rungs to the economic ladder. Although the school mainly transfers its students to four-year colleges, it is increasingly making special efforts for working adults, ages 25 to 45, who want to upskill their way to better pay. The school has created what it calls its "career-express" model—intensive, short bursts of training, in collaboration with nonprofits and companies, that immediately produce a valuable credential.

Administrators learned early on that a traditional academic model—here's a list of classes, now take a few—was ineffective at retaining adult learners. Students were too easily derailed by circumstances like a car breakdown or child-care problem. The school reduced these obstacles by condensing schedules so classes could be completed in a short burst. Students who would struggle to maintain momentum in a two-year degree program are able to add classes to their normal work and home responsibilities for an intensive three- to five-week period. More generally, classes were refocused on the end result most students were seeking: a better job, a better life.

"We tried to understand the value proposition from the student's point of view," says Shugart. "The value proposition has to be about the end result—work—and not about the training itself. They can't see the light at the end of the tunnel. It's too long of a tunnel. But if we take them through a series of very short tunnels, where the opportunity cost of lost wages while they're in school is small, they're perfectly willing to enroll."

Stackable credentials make this practical. Each completed course has immediate value. And students who add more modules down the road can improve their employment prospects even more. In manufacturing, for example, Valencia offers ten certifications, clumped in areas like digital controls, welding, and mechatronics. These are skills local employers have made clear they need immediately. And the more credentials a student piles up, the more they augment their earning power.

In addition to its career express credentialing effort, Valencia offers around 90 associate degree programs in technical fields. Some of the most popular choices including nursing, cardiovascular technology, engineering technologies, entertainment-related technologies, criminal justice, and paralegal studies. Fully 70,000 students are enrolled on six campuses sprinkled across the two-county area surrounding Orlando. Post-graduation services are also big at Valencia. The college works with the local workforce board to try to have a job waiting for every graduating student.

In an interview on one of his campuses, Shugart suggested many ways donors can help community colleges boost career training. One idea is to fund what he terms "SOS" grants. Valencia staff identify serious students who are struggling to pay their bills, and then offer assistance to meet emergency needs, with the goal of ensuring they remain enrolled in school. More generally, Shugart suggests that philanthropists focus on providing the kinds of services that keep people "engaged and afloat" as they pursue training. In Orlando, for instance, Goodwill Industries provides services such as family counseling, housing assistance, career guidance, and substance-abuse mediation, with donor funding.

"A $1 million gift has ten times as much leverage here as it would at some highly branded university," argues Shugart. "Colleges like ours offer a whole lot more leverage on a donation aimed at increasing social mobility."

Red Rocks Community College
Nestled in the shadows of the Rocky Mountains, Red Rocks Community College is the only community college in the nation to offer a master's degree (in medical science), and the only community college in Colorado to offer a bachelor's degree (in water management). The school is a popular choice for transfer students, being the top feeder to the Colorado School of Mines. But it is also carving a niche for career and technical education that leads students directly to real-world applications in the job market.

About 60 percent of Red Rock students are enrolled in CTE programs, including health care, computer technology, business, cosmetology, graphic design, fine woodworking, emergency medical service, fire science, accounting, construction, auto service, and renewable energy trades. There is a special emphasis on STEM instruction. The school has a strong concurrent-enrollment program for high-school students, who can earn credits and even associate degrees when they complete high school.

The college keeps its thumb to the pulse of the local economy. When a local mining company laid off several hundred workers, Red Rocks switched into high gear in early 2016 and offered special CTE options to the displaced employees. "One of the great things about Red Rocks is that we're able to respond to local needs and be nimble," says Ron Slinger, who directs the school's nonprofit foundation. The college has a large career advisory board which meets twice a year to discuss changes in the economy and growing employer needs.

Red Rocks has a special training pathway for individuals transitioning out of prison. The Gateway Program starts ex-offenders with nine credit hours of introductory courses on study skills and career development, and requires a paper in which the person's background, obstacles, and opportunities are assessed. Enrollees then matriculate into the general student population, with the availability of strong support services, including help with transportation and housing. While the three-year recidivism rate for former prisoners is 50 percent nationally, graduates of the Gateway Program are rearrested less than 5 percent of the time.

> Too many donors support only their alma maters and flagship universities, overlooking the immense value that a career-savvy community college can bring to a region.

A sector-wide approach

An ambitious example of several community colleges joining together to cultivate a powerful local workforce comes from the Houston-Galveston region of Texas. Starting in 2013, ExxonMobil offered grants totaling $1.5 million to establish the Community College Petrochemical Initiative. It brings together nine Gulf Coast community colleges to pursue three overarching goals: to convince young people that work in the petrochemical industry is desirable, recruit faculty to teach petrochemical topics (not easy because anyone capable of teaching can earn far more working in the industry), and train enrolled students.

The initiative currently focuses on 14 very specific job types valued in the energy industry. One product of the collaborative is the online site EnergizeHouston.org which provides a detailed listing of the numbers of jobs available at regional energy companies, projected job growth through 2026, and their median pay. These are linked to the fields of study needed to master the job, and information on the nine community colleges offering training.

Recruiting qualified workers in the petrochemical field is reaching emergency status in southeast Texas. An aging workforce is retiring in large numbers, and an estimated $35 billion in future plant expansions is in the works. There may be no other area of the country producing more opportunities for work for individuals willing to acquire specialized skills. "We don't call them jobs. We call them careers, because they last a lifetime and they pay well," explains Dennis Brown, president of Lee College, which leads the collaboration.

There are many ways to invest in community colleges

Although community colleges are public entities, donors have many ways they can invest. Providing infrastructure like a new workshop or industry-standard machines can stimulate much useful activity. Donors can provide scholarships for students who aspire to a technical career but have economic need. They can fund nonprofits that provide wraparound services to students to help them stay enrolled. In some of the more expensive, cutting-edge fields such as biotechnology, regular investments are necessary to keep equipment and training up to date. Some philanthropists may want to help recruit crucial faculty to career-training tracks, to fund career counselors who link students to employers, or to create a job-mapping system that will allow a college to show adult workers how upgrading their skills can lead them to better positions.

Publicizing outstanding career training by a community college can be important in getting other donors over a key hurdle: the tendency of many philanthropists to target only prominent four-year colleges with their grantmaking. Too many donors support only their alma maters and flagship universities, overlooking the immense value that a career-savvy community college can bring to a region. There may be no better instrument available across America today than community colleges when it comes to improving economic mobility—and donors have a key role to play.

Helping Adult Workers to "Upskill"

Many nonprofit organizations and businesses are helping adult workers improve their abilities so they're qualified to thrive in middle-wage jobs. This chapter focuses on such organizations, many of which operate with philanthropic help. Some are quite inventive. Excel Centers, for example, are charter schools operated by regional branches of Goodwill Industries specifically to offer career and technical education to adults who have no high-school diploma and no stable career path. The schools in Indiana and Tennessee, for instance, provide not only detailed career training in scores of different locations, but also a suite of childcare, transportation, coaching, and other services that help students earn not only degrees but also numerous industry certifications. Some student begin postsecondary study as well, via a dual-enrollment option. The Excel Centers offer highly flexible scheduling to make sure the adult enrollees can juggle their education, work, and family responsibilities.

Before sketching some other examples of worthy adult skill training, here are some overarching factors that the dozens of donors, experts, and non-profit practitioners we interviewed for this guidebook told us were important to keep in mind when offering technical education to adult workers.

Clear pathways
Adult workers need a clear vision of the ultimate rewards before venturing into a demanding training program. A career map that clearly shows the benefits associated with various kinds of learning is very helpful.

Condensed time frames and convenient scheduling
Acceleration of coursework is important when dealing with low-income adult workers. A successful model might take what would normally be a nine-month class and condense it to 16 weeks. Low-income workers can't afford to take off most of a year, but they might be able to swing evening classes for four months.

Positive perceptions of postsecondary education
Low-income workers tend to view themselves as unable to successfully swim in the world of postsecondary attainment. Tangibly demonstrating that college success is possible, through models and successful predecessors, can be very helpful.

Special programs for remedial learners
Some adult learners lack basic skills in reading, writing, and arithmetic. Fixing these problems in an accelerated manner while also transmitting core technical skills is something many of the most successful programs have learned to do.

Effective wraparound services
The McKinsey Social Initiative has found that distance to class is the top indicator of whether a new worker will remain on the job. Transportation

obstacles and other practical hurdles can make or break an adult learner's success. These are simple things donors can help with.

Examples from the for-profit world

To see where you as a donor might fit into our nation's system of technical education, let's start by understanding what actions employers are taking to keep their pipelines of talent from running dry.

Trio Electric is a company with 350 employees that does electrical construction for multi-unit buildings in Houston. Major shortages of qualified technicians have pinched the firm's ability to thrive and grow. Historically, it and other electrical installers relied on a trade association to tackle training and recruiting. When more than 60 percent of those recruits started washing out when they hit real jobs, Trio Electric decided to take responsibility for training its own workforce. The company launched a four-year internship program, licensed by the state of Texas, in 2012.

The program has proven effective, both for the company and for the individuals enrolled. "It's a key part of our success," says Beau Pollock, Trio Electric's president. "Houston has a skilled workforce, but it's aging, so we decided to take matters into our own hands."

Training is conducted at the Trio Electric offices, and then on the job. Each year's effort begins with an initial class of about 50 students recruited directly out of high school. To identify eligible candidates, Trio Electric partners with local charter schools run by KIPP and Yes Prep. The fact that enrollees will immediately begin earning a $12/hour wage, rising to $22/hour by the end of the four-year program, is an attractive carrot for many students.

The company made a heavy investment in a curriculum and in developing key performance indicators to keep participants on track. The rate of attrition among its apprentices turned out to be half the level in the wider industry. Trio's trainees are fully prepared for work in approximately half the time it takes a student to go through a traditional classroom environment. They earn a journeyman's license once they've put in around 8,000 hours of on-the-job training and classroom experience.

By 2015, a third of Trio Electric's workforce was enrolled in its apprenticeship program. In the future, Trio Electric plans to turn the apprenticeship program into a separate department of the company and open it to other organizations looking for a way to train employees. The only constraint, Pollock finds, is a lack of awareness among students that the skilled trades provide excellent occupational opportunities today.

Pollock would love to see donors become more involved in funding feeder organizations, such as the KIPP and Yes Prep schools that he relies on. Intelligent grants, he thinks, could both help prepare opportunities for such training educationally, inform students about the chances that middle-skill jobs offer them for life success, and help set up mechanisms for matching apprentices and other new entrants to the work force with employers in need of talent.

> The only constraint is a lack of awareness among students that skilled trades provide excellent opportunities today.

An appealing corporate-nonprofit-foundation partnership that exists today in Dallas links Omni Hotels to a Christian workforce development group called HIS Bridge Builders. The two linked arms when the hotel chain was planning to build a new downtown property and needed to fill a variety of positions. They created a training track that equips low-income, unemployed, or working-poor residents to succeed at hospitality-industry jobs. To date, the program has made more than 135 job placements.

In addition to four to six weeks of training, their model includes on-site job coaching, counseling, mentoring, and income supports. The coaches reduce attrition rates and help the employees stay around long enough to advance in skills and responsibilities.

HIS Bridge Builders operates another training program for ex-offenders. It prepares them to work outdoors with a commercial landscaping company. If the individual referred to them doesn't yet have the basic social capacities for job-holding, HIS Bridge Builders sends them to the Bonton Farms, a nonprofit that provides intensive life-skills training, plus assistance with things like obtaining a driver's license.

While corporations making alliances to provide CTE training are often aiming to fill open positions, the firm Norton Healthcare is mostly aiming to help its entry-level workforce gain the skills needed to move up in the company. As one of the largest health-care providers in Kentucky—with 40 locations and 13,000 employees—Norton particularly hopes that training incumbent workers might help it address shortages in hard-to-fill areas, like qualified nurses. Specifically, the company hopes that the certified nursing assistants it employs as lower-tier staff will consider "credentialing up" to become registered nurses (which could nearly double their wages).

Norton provides multiple pathways to help existing employees rise. It builds its classes around their present work schedules, for instance. The company's commitment to internal employees is one reason Norton Healthcare's five-year employee retention rate is a high 85 percent. "We definitely see a loyalty in those we invest in, and a commitment," says Norton's Jackie Beard.

Nonprofits that prepare workers

We encourage readers here to consult the 2015 Philanthropy Roundtable guidebook *Clearing Obstacles to Work*. Though most of the nonprofit organizations profiled there are focused on securing entry-level work for troubled populations, many—like Cincinnati Works and the Chicago-based Cara Program—have also made job advancement an important part of their efforts. Following are profiles of four charitable organizations that run successful efforts specifically to pull workers up to middle-skill level.

Per Scholas

When it comes to imparting technical knowledge and skills to struggling populations, there are few organizations better known than Per Scholas. Launched two decades ago, its original mission was to bridge the tech divide in the South Bronx. It has since expanded into IT-related workforce development for low-income residents.

Refurbishing old computers was one of the early tasks of the group. This required training six people in computer basics. They all left the nonprofit six months later because they now had skills that qualified them for well-paying private-sector jobs. "We immediately realized there was an opportunity there to create a workforce development program around IT," says president Plinio Ayala. "So we began to solicit input from local employers to see what they needed. We redesigned our entire curriculum."

Per Scholas has expanded to six locations—Atlanta, Cincinnati, Columbus, Dallas, and Washington, D.C., in addition to New York. All offer eight-week training programs that lead to quick job matches (the goal is a placement within 90 days of completing the program).

Successful completion gives the participant an industry-standard CompTIA credential. While serving very poor individuals—90 percent minorities and a third women— Per Scholas maintains a graduation rate of 86 percent. More than 8 out of 10 graduates find technical work right away, at an average starting salary of $39,000, often with benefits. This compares to average annual earnings when participants come in the door of $7,000.

Per Scholas has formed alliances with other nonprofit organizations that assist with wraparound services. And the group's most important partnership is with local employers. Ayala dubs area businesses the organization's "primary customer."

When the Per Scholas branch in the South Bronx learned that local software consulting company Doran Jones planned to offshore 150 software testing jobs, the nonprofit offered an alternative. It partnered with Doran Jones to create a training center, now called the Urban Development Center, and trained 150 workers for placement in the imperiled jobs. Salaries for the graduates began at $35,000 per year and jumped to $50,000 the second year.

Per Scholas has attracted philanthropic support from major foundations and corporations including the Robin Hood, Pinkerton, Tiger, and Kellogg foundations, New York City Workforce Funders, Capital One, and JPMorgan Chase. JPMC donated close to $1 million five years ago to launch the expansion of Per Scholas nationwide. The financial services firm Barclays has also made major cash gifts in recent years, and provided upward of 200 volunteers per year to the nonprofit.

Brooklyn Workforce Innovations

Brooklyn Workforce Innovations helps jobless or low-income New Yorkers find family-sustaining careers. And it does this within walking distance of some of the roughest neighborhoods in the five boroughs of New York City. BWI doesn't just focus on helping workers get a job—it aims for placements where steady upward growth of responsibility and wages is possible.

BWI training allows the student to obtain industry-recognized credentials, and then two years of job-placement and career services. Instruction in conflict resolution, networking, and customer service is included to make graduates well-rounded and ready for work. The group recruits from all five boroughs and looks for people who are trainable and motivated to work. The nonprofit culls around 700 trainees from about 5,000 annual applicants. The selection can be rigorous and includes an interview, try-outs (a day or two in a training-like environment to make sure they are well suited), and in some cases homework assignments and drug tests.

BWI currently provides four sector-based training programs and one general job certification:

- *Brooklyn Networks* trains participants to install telecom cable. It runs for five weeks and leads to certification in low-voltage installation, equipping graduates to install telephone and computer lines, entertainment systems, and security networks.
- *Brooklyn Woods* provides seven weeks of training in woodworking and cabinetmaking. It cycles through five classes each year.
- *Made in NY* offers five weeks of training for careers in TV and film, leading to a certificate from the New York City Major's Office of Film, Theatre, and Broadcasting, plus two years of job placement assistance.
- *Red Hook on the Road* is a commercial driving class. Four weeks of training leads to a professional license good for trucks, school buses, and airport shuttles.
- *New York Drives* helps participants get a state driver's license so that isn't a career obstacle.

In its latest year, BWI graduated 94 percent of students, resulting in 592 new hires and a 305 percent average wage boost. The nonprofit enjoys strong donor support from groups like the Gimbel, Price Family, Weinberg, Robin Hood, Capital One, RealNetworks, Tiger, and Brooklyn Community foundations.

BioTechnical Institute of Maryland

A prime example of a nonprofit using a potent economic sector—health care—to draw struggling populations into viable work is the BioTechnical Institute of Maryland. It was founded in 1998 to meet growing unmet demand in Baltimore for entry-level biotechnology workers. The program targeted single mothers in their late 20s or early 30s. Seventy percent of participants arrive at BTI's doors either unemployed or underemployed, and 93 percent of its students are minorities.

BTI has developed a robust pre-training program that instructs in professionalism at work, math skills, and basic technical terminology and information. Then there are ten weeks of training in essential laboratory skills. Finally, participants are placed in an internship that encompasses 100 hours of work at a local employer, with BTI covering the costs of the internship. Participating employers often end up hiring the lab interns. On average, BTI graduates expect a starting salary in the range of $28,000 per year, which for the median participant is a 200 percent increase in income.

BTI also offers graduates refresher training and more advanced instruction through its social enterprise, BioSci Concepts. "We're always looking to emphasize to our participants and graduates that we don't want this program to be an end. We want it to be the beginning of their continued academic and professional development," says BTI director Kathleen Weiss.

> We are adamant that our training should be directly related to what employers are looking for.

Many graduates eventually pursue subsequent credentials or post-secondary education. The BTI program alone entitles participants six credit hours toward an associate degree in biotechnology from Baltimore City Community College. The U.S. Bureau of Labor Statistics reports that a typical biological technician with an associate degree earned $41,290 in 2014.

Critical early support for BTI came from the Baltimore-based Abell Foundation, which funds workforce development as one of its core areas. Other mainstay supporters include the Charles Bauer, Casey, Weinberg, and Wells Fargo foundations. "We believe strongly in the model of training city residents in response to local demand for entry-level bio-technicians," says Marci Hunn of the Weinberg Foundation.

Baltimore Alliance for Careers in Healthcare
Another effective nonprofit located in the Charm City is the Baltimore Alliance for Careers in Healthcare, which works with seven city hospitals to identify worker shortages and fill those positions. BACH does not provide training directly. Instead the group works

with area nonprofits, community colleges, and employers to train men and women it has recruited and screened.

"We are adamant that our training should be directly related to what employers are looking for," says BACH executive director Laura Spada. "So we are constantly talking to our community partners about training that is current and in-demand."

The organization mainly focuses on filling posts for medical laboratory technicians, nursing assistants, nurse extenders, pharmacy technicians, radiologic technicians, surgical technologists, and respiratory therapists. In the latest year, the program successfully placed 135 candidates in jobs. BACH has also fine-tuned a career-mapping system that shows workers, in vivid detail, the steps needed to advance from entry- to mid- to high-level positions in the medical field—exactly what credentials and education will be needed for each step, and the pay increases that can be expected. Spada says her organization's career maps are used by high-school guidance counselors to advise students on vocational paths, and by career coaches in hospitals who help existing employees upskill.

Like the BioTechnical Institute, BACH works primarily with minority populations, about two thirds of whom are older single mothers with school-age children. Supported by a number of local philanthropies—including the Weinberg, Abell, and Casey foundations—BACH is looking to expand its reach to new populations in the near future. Marci Hunn of Weinberg admires the program for helping employees, employers, and patients alike. "BACH provides healthcare workers with opportunities for advancement and wage increases. It improves employee retention at job sites. And it produces better patient care outcomes."

Connecting adult learners to the jobs of the future

Workers who excel in the future will often be those who mesh comfortably with technology and machines, argues economist Tyler Cowen in his 2014 book *Average is Over: Powering America Beyond the Age of the Great Stagnation*. As we've explored in this chapter, CTE training is a prime route to those types of jobs. Training for adults has the potential to improve the national economy, transform individuals, and reinvigorate entire families. It can strengthen marriages, give children more stable homes, and strengthen neighborhoods. It can also reduce strident political debate over economic inequality and fair wages by significantly lifting the economic prospects of all Americans.

What role might you play as a donor? Bringing your creativity to bear in this arena could yield significant dividends. In our final chapter we will offer some ideas to spark your thinking.

Sample Investment Opportunities

The United States is currently struggling with depressed rates of labor-force participation. There are 11 million underemployed adults, 7 million youths disconnected from work, and damaging shortages of high-value workers across a range of industries. Excellent career and technical education can salve all of these wounds.

And with work being the starting point for so many other kinds of success, it is hard to think of a more fertile ground for philanthropists who want to aid struggling neighbors than career and technical education.

A simple start could be had in many instances simply by redirecting resources currently being poured into conventional school or college grants. There are many local nonprofits that can be invested in. A donor's business might be used to create apprenticeship or internship opportunities. Alliances with business associations and community colleges hold great promise. There are national models that could be transferred to your local scene—or vice versa. Philanthropists with a taste for organizing and leadership might use their influence to draw together companies, schools, and charities.

"One of the things that makes CTE work so very exciting is that initiatives can be organized in any number of ways—by corporations, by schools, or by nonprofits," notes Lucretia Murphy of Jobs for the Future. Over the past decade, nonprofits have learned valuable lessons about connecting needy populations with labor-force needs in their local communities. Realistic educators are understanding the power of CTE pathways to attract and hold students who are either more ambitious or less corrigible than average. Corporations are realizing how vital it is that they make sure there will be future employees capable of doing their crucial work in adequate numbers. When these various entities cooperate—often with the lubricant of philanthropy—accomplishments of high value to many parties become possible.

Following are some sample ways that you as a donor could take an immediate, useful role in career and technical education.

Investments under $50,000

- **Fund CTE scholarships**
  Follow in the footsteps of former Intel co-founder Andrew Grove. He sponsored community-college scholarships ranging from $500 to $5,000 specifically for students who wanted to transition to a technical job in the workforce rather than continue on to four-year college. He typically gave out 100 scholarships per year.

- **Invest in internships, apprenticeships, and real-world workforce exposures**
  "The heart of effective CTE is work experience," write Tamar Jacoby and Shaun Dougherty in a recent Manhattan Institute report. Tap into

your economic networks to fund company internships, create apprenticeships, or support existing programs. The need is significant: A recent survey by Accenture found that only 41 percent of companies offer any type of internship or apprenticeship for middle-skill jobs.

- **Ensure that CTE students still receive a broad education**
While emphasizing practical job skills, good CTE programs also offer other elements of a well-rounded education. Donors can help fill out CTE programs by helping them create the base academic instruction that students need.

- **Fund essential soft skills training and moral education**
Just as academics can't be sacrificed, neither can soft skills training—the practical attributes of punctuality, diligence, and work ethic. CTE students must be able to think critically and function socially on the job. The value of technical training is muted without the underpinning of strong soft skills. Invest in schools that teach character, morals, and ethical behavior, skills conducive to a good life.

- **Partner with a small company in your area**
Identify a CTE-rich economic sector in your geographic region and find a small company that lacks capacity to pay apprentices. Collaborate with them to fund a joint program that pays youths to apprentice while pursuing a two-year degree from a local community college. Target this initiative to low-income young people.

- **Fill tuition gaps for veterans at community colleges**
As pointed out by Red Rocks Community College president Michele Haney, some veterans experience delays in receiving tuition assistance from the G.I. Bill, or funding gaps between programs or semesters that make it hard for them to stay on degree tracks. "We're constantly looking for emergency funding for vets," says Haney. "How do we take them over from one semester to the next? It becomes a real serious situation for them." Bridge this gap with grants to a community college's foundation.

- **Open alternatives in donor minds to the college-for-all mentality**
  Something as simple as sponsoring a visit to a local CTE program or community college so local philanthropists can see firsthand the value of CTE training could be useful here.

- **Give a CTE grant to a community college's foundation**
  Many community colleges have nonprofit foundations attached that accept grants. This can be a prime entry point for donors wishing to make a difference in these crucial local schools. Identify the best attributes of CTE training at your local community college and consider earmarking funding for it through the foundation.

> Realistic educators are understanding the power of vocational pathways to attract and hold students who are either more ambitious or less corrigible than average.

- **Support Project Lead The Way and other STEM initiatives in public and charter schools**
  PLTW is a proven success. But don't limit your thinking. There may be other options for supporting STEM education in your local schools.

- **Educate community leaders on modern manufacturing**
  Manufacturing is changing rapidly in many industries, and modern firms have very specific needs that ought to be meshed with our education system. The Benedum Foundation has offered grants to support a communications plan known as Explore the New Faces of Manufacturing.

- **Help a nonprofit partner collaborate with a corporate initiative**
  There are many examples. Goodwill of Southwestern Pennsylvania, for instance, has teamed up with the McKinsey Social Initiative's Generation USA program to provide middle-skill jobs training.

Donors could make a grant to Goodwill to help support this effort and others like it.

- **Provide seed funds for a pilot project**
  The Achelis and Bodman Foundations seeded the Woodlawn Cemetery Preservation Training Program with a $30,000 grant. "We were attracted to the program because it's still in the pilot stage, and our funds are perhaps most useful in the early stages when a new idea is being tested and other donors are wariest. In later years when a program is running well, it has less trouble attracting support," notes director John Krieger.

- **Purchase Career Cruising software for a school or nonprofit**
  This is a simple, low-cost way to help students begin thinking about vocation at an early age.

- **Serve on the board of a CTE-oriented nonprofit**
  Apply your expertise and experience to help a workforce nonprofit be more effective.

Investments of $50,000 to $250,000

- **Improve the image of career and technical education**
  CTE runs up against lots of old stigmas about vocational instruction, school "tracking," and second-rate education. Help trumpet the myriad successes of the new brands of technical training, and particularly the importance of "middle-skill" instruction. Funding publications, newspaper editorials, blogging, and research can all help spread the word. Also consider supporting the Association for Career & Technical Education, or one of its state affiliates. These organizations promote the importance of career-oriented education. "Donors can play a role in elevating CTE, making it less of a fall back or career pathway for less capable students," says Carrie Hauser, president of Colorado Mountain College.

- **Fund a robust evaluation tool for CTE programs**
  One obstacle to the spread of CTE initiatives today is that few evaluation methods exist. Donors can help schools, nonprofits,

and partnerships better measure and assess their programs. The Corporation for a Skilled Workforce offers a benchmark report, evaluating workforce development groups, which might be used as a starting point.

- **Fund services, coaches, and mentors that back up CTE instruction**

    Many successful CTE programs rely on support measures that help stressed lower-level workers jump hurdles as they improve their skills for greater success in the future. Your local CTE efforts may need these kinds of supports. This is a very helpful niche for philanthropy to fill.

- **Invest in feeder schools**

    Good CTE programs need good candidates coming out of high schools. Trio Electric's connection to KIPP and YES Prep charter schools in Houston was crucial to the success of their effort. Consider supporting schools that develop the right candidates.

- **Fund hard-to-fill faculty positions**

    It can be difficult to keep faculty positions filled for in-demand technical subjects. Experts well-positioned to teach can often earn significantly more at job sites, and existing teachers can sometimes let their technical skills slip and lose touch with the latest techniques employed in the marketplace. Consider creating a specific fund to support recruitment and salaries for such positions, and for helping existing faculty increase their knowledge of the latest technologies and approaches.

- **Create prizes for outstanding CTE programs**

    Like the Aspen Institute's annual rankings of the most excellent community colleges, create a prize for CTE programs that excel.

- **Promote flexibility in CTE instruction**

    Georgetown University's *Failure to Launch* report urges that flexible class times, along with paid internships, fellowships, and apprenticeships, "help young adults balance competing work and education demands." Don't make candidates fit the mold; reshape the mold to fit them if you want to avoid high dropout rates.

- **Help schools keep ahead of the technology curve**
  Consider investments that allow a local school or nonprofit to update its buildings, software, and machines to make certain students are being trained at the state of the art.

Investments of $250,000 to $1 million

- **Help schools and employers forge alliances**
  Break down barriers between educational institutions and employers. Encourage employers to better identify their talent needs, and push educational institutions not to worry that they will lose their academic independence if they tailor programs that bring students and jobs together.

> Don't make candidates fit the mold; reshape the mold to fit them if you want to avoid high dropout rates.

- **Expand the vision of your alma mater**
  Work with your alma matter (or universities and colleges in general) to do a better job of linking graduates with jobs. Accenture research shows that just 4 percent of job seekers say that schools and universities are the best source of information on job opportunities. And encourage four-year colleges and universities not to neglect new technical fields (like in many branches of computer programming) where multiyear education is needed and there are far too few graduates to meet economic demand.

- **Help entry-level workers jump to the next level**
  Countless nonprofits across the country do a stellar job of taking individuals without a successful economic history and showing them how to succeed in entry-level jobs. There is much less philanthropic work taking place, however, to help low-level workers improve their skills to a middle level. Earmark funding specifically to help a worthy workforce nonprofit make this significant jump.

- **Invest to improve graduation rates at two-year colleges**
  This would pay many benefits, to students and the national economy alike. It will require better screening, improved adult basic education, improved counseling and coaching, cost control, more roadmapping of degree paths, and improved support services.

- **Endow a scholarship at a community college to reach a specific subpopulation**
  If your giving is oriented around a particular subpopulation—such as veterans or students with STEM talents, or ex-prisoners—consider endowing a scholarship at a community college with solid CTE programs, aimed at that specific population.

- **Fund a national or regional association that helps CTE educators and the organizers of middle-skill jobs initiatives collaborate**
  Set up a mechanism that helps participants gather on a regular basis, share ideas, and set long-term priorities.

- **Fund a CTE curriculum at a community college or technical school**
  Following the example of donor Karen Buchwald Wright and the Ariel Corporation, create a CTE curriculum in schools in your geographic location.

Investments of $1 million or more

- **Create a major database of unfilled jobs and correlate it with available or needed CTE training**
  A major obstacle to successful CTE program is ignorance about the plentiful job opportunities available in technical and trade fields. As suggested by the McKinsey Global Institute, creating a national database showing what jobs are most in demand (and where) would be of incredible use. Similarly, a Georgetown University report recommends creating a learning and earning exchange, an "information system that links high-school and postsecondary transcript information about courses taken and

grades with employer wage records. Such a system would allow all to see how successful various programs are at producing job-ready graduates."

- **Help a successful local organization expand nationally**
  Groups like Per Scholas have already made the leap from local to national activity. Provide the funding to take other nonprofits or schools to a wide audience.

- **Launch a foundation at your local community college**
  Locate a community college in your area that is effective at career education. If the institution doesn't already have a foundation, provide the seed money for starting one. Such foundations are often important in launching new job-linking ventures.

- **Make CTE a part of broader higher education reforms**
  Postsecondary reforms tend to focus mainly on four-year schools, but you as a donor can work to ensure that two-year schools and certification programs aren't left out of the discussion.

Donors have a powerful role to play in the rise of career and technical education, and they can begin right in their backyards. Your own alma mater, your local community college, nearby schools, the workforce-development nonprofits that exist in most counties, regional businesses hungry for partners who can help them solve crippling skill shortages—these institutions can often become successful partners in transitioning workers from lower-skill work into vocations that offer stable middle-class wages.

There is a delightful paradox in helping people qualify for middle-skill jobs. Philanthropic support for education that helps people become economically mobile unquestionably qualifies as a charitable good. At the same time, it makes practical business and economic sense. Investing in widening and strengthening the job-talent pipeline is a victory for all.

INDEX

ABOUT THE PHILANTHROPY ROUNDTABLE

The Philanthropy Roundtable is America's leading network of charitable donors working to strengthen our free society, uphold donor intent, and protect the freedom to give. Our members include individual philanthropists, families, corporations, and private foundations.

Mission

The Philanthropy Roundtable's mission is to foster excellence in philanthropy, to protect philanthropic freedom, to assist donors in achieving their philanthropic intent, and to help donors advance liberty, opportunity, and personal responsibility in America and abroad.

Principles

- Philanthropic freedom is essential to a free society
- A vibrant private sector generates the wealth that makes philanthropy possible
- Voluntary private action offers solutions to many of society's most pressing challenges
- Excellence in philanthropy is measured by results, not by good intentions
- A respect for donor intent is essential to long-term philanthropic success

Services

World-class conferences

The Philanthropy Roundtable connects you with other savvy donors. Held across the nation throughout the year, our meetings assemble grantmakers and experts to develop strategies for excellent local, state, and national giving. You will hear from innovators in K–12 education, economic opportunity, higher education, national security, and other fields. Our Annual Meeting is the Roundtable's flagship event, gathering the nation's most public-spirited and influential philanthropists for debates, how-to sessions, and discussions on the best ways for private individuals to achieve powerful results through their giving. The Annual Meeting is a stimulating and enjoyable way to meet principled donors seeking the breakthroughs that can solve our nation's greatest challenges.

Breakthrough groups
Our Breakthrough groups—focused program areas—build a critical mass of donors around a topic where dramatic results are within reach. Breakthrough groups become a springboard to help donors achieve lasting effects from their philanthropy. Our specialized staff of experts helps grantmakers invest with care in areas like anti-poverty work, philanthropy for veterans, and family reinforcement. The Roundtable's K–12 education program is our largest and longest-running Breakthrough group. This network helps donors zero in on today's most promising school reforms. We are the industry-leading convener for philanthropists seeking systemic improvements through competition and parental choice, administrative freedom and accountability, student-centered technology, enhanced teaching and school leadership, and high standards and expectations for students of all backgrounds. We foster productive collaboration among donors of varied ideological perspectives who are united by a devotion to educational excellence.

A powerful voice
The Roundtable's public-policy project, the Alliance for Charitable Reform (ACR), works to advance the principles and preserve the rights of private giving. ACR educates legislators and policymakers about the central role of charitable giving in American life and the crucial importance of protecting philanthropic freedom—the ability of individuals and private organizations to determine how and where to direct their charitable assets. Active in Washington, D.C., and in the states, ACR protects charitable giving, defends the diversity of charitable causes, and battles intrusive government regulation. We believe the capacity of private initiative to address national problems must not be burdened with costly or crippling constraints.

Protection of donor interests
The Philanthropy Roundtable is the leading force in American philanthropy to protect donor intent. Generous givers want assurance that their money will be used for the specific charitable aims and purposes they

believe in, not redirected to some other agenda. Unfortunately, donor intent is usually violated in increments, as foundation staff and trustees neglect or misconstrue the founder's values and drift into other purposes. Through education, practical guidance, legislative action, and individual consultation. The Philanthropy Roundtable is active in guarding donor intent. We are happy to advise you on steps you can take to ensure that your mission and goals are protected.

Must-read publications
Philanthropy, the Roundtable's quarterly magazine, is packed with useful and beautifully written real-life stories. It offers practical examples, inspiration, detailed information, history, and clear guidance on the differences between giving that is great and giving that disappoints.

We also publish a series of guidebooks that provide detailed information on the very best ways to be effective in particular aspects of philanthropy. These guidebooks are compact, brisk, and readable. Most focus on one particular area of giving—for instance, how to improve teaching, charter school expansion, support for veterans, programs that get the poor into jobs, how to invest in public policy, and other topics of interest to grantmakers. Real-life examples, hard numbers, first-hand experiences of other donors, recent history, and policy guidance are presented to inform and inspire savvy donors.

The Roundtable's *Almanac of American Philanthropy* is the definitive reference book on private giving in our country. It profiles America's greatest givers (historic and current), describes the 1,000 most consequential philanthropic achievements since our founding, and compiles comprehensive statistics on the field. Our *Almanac* summarizes the major books, key articles, and most potent ideas animating U.S. philanthropy. It includes a 23-page timeline, national poll, legal analysis, and other crucial—and fascinating—finger-tip facts on this vital piece of American culture.

Join the Roundtable!
When working with The Philanthropy Roundtable, members are better equipped to achieve long-lasting success with their charitable giving. Your membership in the Roundtable will make you part of a potent network that understands philanthropy and strengthens our free society. Philanthropy Roundtable members range from Forbes 400 individual givers and the largest American foundations to small family

foundations and donors just beginning their charitable careers. Our members include:

- Individuals and families
- Private foundations
- Community foundations
- Venture philanthropists
- Corporate giving programs
- Large operating foundations and charities that devote more than half of their budget to external grants

Philanthropists who contribute at least $100,000 annually to charitable causes are eligible to become members of the Roundtable and register for most of our programs. Roundtable events provide you with a solicitation-free environment.

For more information on The Philanthropy Roundtable or to learn about our individual program areas, please call (202) 822-8333 or e-mail main@PhilanthropyRoundtable.org.

ABOUT THE AUTHOR

David Bass is author of the 2015 Philanthropy Roundtable guidebook *Clearing Obstacles to Work: A Wise Giver's Guide to Fostering Self-Reliance.* He previously served at the John William Pope Foundation in North Carolina, where he focused on nonprofits involved in workforce development. He has a journalism degree from Thomas Edison State College, and lives with his wife in North Carolina, where he operates a consulting firm specializing in communications and writing.